Life's Journey

on a magic carpet

Ian Swart

First published by Busybird Publishing 2024

Copyright © 2024 Ian Swart

ISBN:
Paperback: 978-1-923216-66-2
Ebook: 978-1-923216-67-9

This work is copyright. Apart from any use permitted under the *Copyright Act 1968*, no part of this publication may be reproduced, stored in a retrieval system or transmitted in any form or by any means, electronic, mechanical, photocopying, recording or otherwise, without the prior written permission of Ian Swart.

The information in this book is based on the author's experiences and opinions. The author and publisher disclaim responsibility for any adverse consequences, which may result from use of the information contained herein. Permission to use any external content has been sought by the author. Any breaches will be rectified in further editions of the book.

Cover design: Elijah Swart

Layout and typesetting: Busybird Publishing

Busybird Publishing
2/118 Para Road
Montmorency, Victoria
Australia 3094
www.busybird.com.au

Preface

This memoir is about my other life. The one my family and friends do not really know about or have only heard fragments.

These are the times I have spent overseas, the adventures, the friends I have made during my travels, a series of sliding door moments and the funny experiences I have encountered whilst establishing a successful family-run carpet business.

My story threads its way through my life from the time I spent in the fashion industry, my journey as a hippie through which time I always maintained a flair for fashion and how a family tragedy pushed me into the world of handmade rugs, eventually opening retail stores nationally in Australia called Hali Handmade Carpets. I changed the industry by introducing fashion via colour into traditional rugs and curating rug ranges specifically for Australia, steering the rug industry into a new course. It has been a great adventure and I feel very privileged and lucky to have experienced this journey. It is something that is not possible today. Times have changed. Today, you cannot travel overland like I did in the 1970s and my experiences in India, especially in my early days of establishing contacts in the rug industry, are not possible due to the changes that emanate.

My son Dan is a member of the Entrepreneurs Organisation (EO) and is the managing director of Hali Handmade Carpets, the company I started in 1983. In 2023, he asked me to give a speech to his local EO chapter about my life in the late sixties and seventies in which I was part of the hippie culture, my overland travels on the hippie trail, my love of India and how it led me into a world of rugs and the establishment of my carpet business. They loved listening to my speech and thought that I had lived during a fascinating time and that my life journey was a story to be told.

I showed the speech to my wife Gina, my children, my brother and his wife Fay, his son Elliot and a close friend Peter who is a motivational speaker. They were all in awe of it as they were unaware of the many experiences I had encountered throughout my life.

I also showed it to my gym group and received a similar reaction notably from my friend Phillip who wrote, 'Irene and I have just read your speech. It is the most delightful read and I actually have a tear in my eye as it is a beautiful story. It is amazing how much can be achieved in a lifetime. It is also amazing that we have known each other for a long time but there is so much there that I didn't know. We both encourage you to expand and keep writing as the era and your journey make interesting and delightful reading.'

The reaction from my family and friends and the disappointment that my grandfather Isadore didn't write his story for all to share are the motivation for me writing the following memoir so that current and future generations can read my journey. The life I have led can never be repeated as the world is forever evolving and each generation experiences something different.

I hope you enjoy reading my memoir as much as I have enjoyed writing it, something I never dreamed I could do or ever considered.

PART ONE

Chapter 1

Rugs and travel have always been in my blood.

My father, Louis, opened a small Persian rug shop in Toorak Rd South Yarra in 1974. He was experienced in selling Persian carpets as he had done so in South Africa during the 1930s. Born in Amsterdam in 1910, he decided to travel the world starting in South Africa at the tender age of twenty-two, where he first worked in the diamond trade (he was a diamond cutter in Amsterdam) before venturing into Persian Carpet sales. He spent several years in South Africa plus time in New Zealand before settling in Australia in 1939. He never returned to Amsterdam or saw his family again as the Second World War had begun. Amsterdam was invaded by Germany and his entire family, parents, brother, younger sister and all his cousins died in concentration camps. One second cousin, a young boy named Sam Wennek, is the only member of his family who survived the Holocaust. My father also had one cousin, Cato, who had fortunately migrated to Sydney in the 1930s, therefore missing the holocaust. They remained close.

I researched my father's family several years ago on the Yad Vashem website in Israel and traced fifty of his close relatives all exterminated in the camps mainly in the Sobibor Concentration Camp. Thirty-five thousand Dutch Jews were sent to Sobibor; only eighteen survived.

After the war, in the late 1940s and 1950s, he would travel to the countryside in Victoria with a boot and car full of Belgian machine-made Persian design rugs selling them to farmers and country townspeople. The importer of these rugs was his father-in-law, my grandfather Isadore. Isadore had connections in Antwerp and imported these rugs to

Australia selling them to carpet stores in the major cities. These carpets were not available in the countryside so several of the 'Dutch Boys', as they called themselves, would get stock from him weekly and travel to the countryside my father and uncle Coenie, my mother's brother, included. Coenie opened a Persian rug shop in the 1960s at the Southern Cross Hotel in the City of Melbourne.

My parents met in Melbourne in 1940 through the Dutch Jewish community that was prevalent at the time and of which my parents remained part. During the war, my father served as a Sergeant Major in the Dutch Australian Army. Whilst in service in 1942, he married my mother; my brother Nick was born in 1943.

My mother, Sylvia, also came from a Dutch background. Her mother, Carolina, was born in Rotterdam and travelled with her parents to New York at the young age of sixteen where she worked in a music store. My grandfather, Isadore van Embden, was born in Antwerp Belgium to Dutch parents and also travelled to New York where he met my grandmother. They married in 1913 when my grandmother was seventeen and soon after, moved to San Francisco where their first son Joseph was born. From there, they moved to London. My mother was born in London and when she was four years of age, they moved to Antwerp for a few years and on to Cape Town where my mother's younger brother Coenie was born. They then moved back to Antwerp before escaping the Nazis in 1939 on a ship to Australia and settling in Melbourne. My grandfather's siblings all escaped the war by moving to Cape Town during the 1930s.

I'm not sure what work my grandfather did in these cities but had heard whilst growing up that he had businesses in pinball machines, diamonds and Persian carpets. Many years after he passed away, my uncle told me the most fascinating story. 'In 1936, my grandfather Isadore travelled from Antwerp to Persia, bought a truckload of Persian carpets, drove in a convoy overland to India and travelled throughout India selling the carpets to the Maharajahs and to the British Raj.'

He never documented his travels from Persia nor about his life after having lived in Antwerp, New York, San Francisco, London, Cape Town and Melbourne. The only mode of travel being by ship. What an interesting life he must have led and how remiss of him never to write anything down so that future generations could read of his experiences.

My grandfather had a heart attack in his late forties and became scared of his future so he closed his business and stopped working. To keep the income flowing my grandmother took up the reins and started selling rugs. She had a stack of the Belgium rugs in their garage at the apartment they lived in in Ripponlea, would advertise in the classified section of the newspapers and there she was, another family member selling Persian-style rugs.

Chapter 2

My flare for fashion began when I was very young. I don't really know why I was interested in fashion at this early age. It was possibly an influence by my mother, who was a very stylish and fashionable lady. Mum would dress up to go to the City often wearing a tailored suit with a slim fitting jacket, a silky blouse and a straight skirt, accessorised by gloves, pointy patent shoes and matching handbag. She would often take me along with her to the city stores where she carefully selected outfits for herself. Her more casual daily look was to wear a fitted sweater or cardigan paired with a matching skirt.

I started my first job at the age of eight working in a menswear store in Glenhuntly Rd Elwood, which was down the road from the two-bedroom flat where I lived with my parents and older brother. The owner was a lovely gentleman named Mr Walker. I would often go and see him after school and hang around his store. Mr Walker was a kind man with a fine moustache and thick glasses. He always wore a shirt and tie with a sleeveless V-neck pullover. To be nice to me, he allowed me to work in his shop on Saturday mornings. It wasn't really a job and I'm sure I wasn't paid but he made a little boy very happy. Mr Walker allowed me to sell gloves and hankies. Standing behind the counter was my big thrill! I would keep rearranging and straightening the gloves, which were neatly placed in a drawer under the glass top counter. The hankies were kept separately in a wooden box on a shelf behind me. It was only a small store with terrible lighting and a musty smell, which didn't bother me as I just loved being surrounded by the clothing he had on display. I don't remember his shop ever being very busy.

At age fourteen, I started working during the school holidays at Chesters Menswear at the Southern Cross Hotel in the City of Melbourne, which, at the time, was Melbourne's number-one men's fashion store. The store was owned by Jack Vigushin, a friend of my father's. Being only fourteen, I was employed as an assistant to fold shirts, knitwear, jackets, trousers, etc. and place them back on the shelves after the salespeople finished showing. When the salespeople were all serving, I would try to assist customers. I was good, very good, and often outsold the senior salespeople. It wasn't long before Jack told me to not bother folding the stock and putting them back but to sell, sell, sell. I became one of Chesters top salespeople and Jack was hoping that after I finished school, I would become a fulltime salesman at Chesters. Sorry, Jack, but it was never on my radar!

When I was seventeen, Jack opened a small exclusive store on Swanston Street, which his son, Tom ran. During school holidays and Saturday mornings, I would work with Tom. On the weekend, stores were open on Saturday mornings only and not open on Sundays, so it was usually very busy. I loved my selling experience at Chesters and continued working there part-time until I was twenty-three.

My schooling was at Caulfield Grammar School and in 1968, I attended Monash University to study law. Given a choice, I would probably have entered the fashion industry but with peer pressure, my parents' insistence and being a good Jewish boy, I went to university to study law.

University was very different in the late 1960s. There were no online lectures, so we would spend our day on campus to attend lectures and tutorials. For me, it was mostly socialising in the cafeteria!

On Fridays, there were concerts that were popular with the students and contributed to the vibrant music scene of the era. There were performances by folk musicians, rock bands and blues artists. Some of these musicians who appeared got their start at Monash as it was popular for local artists to gain exposure. Some went on to achieve national and international recognition such as Billy Thorpe and the Aztecs, Max Merritt and the Meteors, the Easybeats, the Masters Apprentices and the Twilights.

Monash also held a weekly flea market organised and run by students – this was a significant aspect of campus life at the time. They often had musicians and street performers adding to its lively vibe and it provided an opportunity for students to sell items such as clothing, books, records and other personal items that they no longer needed. As well as these second-hand items, local artisans and students could sell their handmade crafts, art or other creative products.

This was the time of a changing world and Monash students were actively involved in various protest movements such as opposing the Vietnam War, supporting socialism, demonstrating against Apartheid in South Africa, and in support of women's rights and the 1968 Civil Rights movement after the assassination of Martin Luther King. The largest influence on students in the 1960s was the Flower Power Movement. It began in the mid-1960s in San Francisco and spread throughout the USA and internationally. This movement was one of nonviolence, love and compassion, peace and harmony and rejecting conformity. It called for peaceful resolutions to all conflicts and, especially at that time, the Vietnam War. It was closely aligned with the hippie counterculture, which embraced alternative lifestyles, community and communal living, environmentalism and a rejection of materialism and consumerism advocating for social change.

People adorned themselves with flowers, often distributing them as a symbol of peace and unity. I had colourful stick-on flowers covering the rust on my first car a 1960 Fiat 1100, which I bought for $200.

The Beatles were influential in the Flower Power and hippie movement due to their music, lyrics and their changing appearance. Songs such as *All You Need is Love, Strawberry Fields Forever* and *Lucy in the Sky with Diamonds* became anthems for this counterculture. In addition to their music, The Beatles' experimentation with psychedelic drugs and especially smoking marijuana became a symbol of rebellion. Their openness about using marijuana was widely embraced and helped destigmatise the drug and contributed to its integration into lifestyle. Their influence in fashion, art and social attitudes helped shape the cultural landscape of this era, leaving a lasting legacy for generations following.

The Beatles became a great influence on my life. I loved their music and still do. The influence they had on society with the Flower Power Movement set me on the road to becoming a hippie with its ideals about peace, love, personal freedom and social equality. I wore colourful shirts, flared pants and platform shoes, grew a moustache (which I still have), grew my hair long (which I am no longer able to do) and became a regular smoker of marijuana. I was fortunate to see The Beatles live in 1964 at Festival Hall when I was fourteen. My older brother, Nick took me; it was my first ever concert.

The rock musical *Hair* was released in 1968 and was known for its integration of rock music and sexual revolution embracing long hair, free love, flower power and psychedelic drugs. Songs such as *Aquarius, Let the Sunshine In* and *Good Morning Starshine* became iconic anthems of the era.

Woodstock was a three-day music festival held in New York State in 1969 attended by 400,000 peace-loving attendees exemplifying the ideals of peace, love and harmony espoused by the hippie movement. In 1972, the Sunbury Music Festival was held in Australia, emulating Woodstock.

The hippie movement was a changing time in the world. I was there. I was part of it and very lucky to have been the right age at this time.

The Vietnam War was in full force and back in 1964, the Australian Government had introduced the National Service Act requiring males of twenty years of age to serve twenty-four months of full-time service followed by three years in the reserve if selected in the ballot. Two ballots were conducted each year. The ballot was conducted using a lottery barrel and marbles representing birthdays and if your corresponding birthday was selected, you were called up for National Service with the possibility of being posted in Vietnam during its war with Australia, USA and many other countries.

Coming home one afternoon in late 1969, my mother was sitting at the kitchen table waiting for me with a letter in front of her from the Department of Labour and National Service. I nervously opened it and it read: 'This is to advise you that you have been granted indefinite deferment of your liability to render national service, and consequently, under present arrangements, you will not be called up.' What a great relief that was – my birthday had not been selected in the ballot.

In 1969, my second year at Monash, a friend of my father's had imported a product from China but didn't have any salespeople on the road, so I took on a part time job with him, which was commission based. The product was a mini shopping bag that stretched. It looked like a hair net with handles. As you placed your goods in from the supermarket, it stretched and accommodated most of your shopping. It was quite a novel product. I would approach independent supermarkets and set up a stand with a sign. Each week, I would go back, refill and invoice for those sold.

During the summer holidays in 1969, I went to Sydney and met two young, very stylish Frenchmen who were producing a beautiful range of young women's sportswear, which they were selling successfully in Sydney but had no representation in Melbourne, so I took on their agency for Victoria. The range was called Michelle Lucien and I had a lot of fun and success selling it to fashion boutiques in Melbourne throughout my third year of law at Monash.

On May 8th 1970, during my third year of law, I marched in the Moratorium, which opposed Australia's involvement in the Vietnam War, and demanded the withdrawal of Australian troops and the abolishment of conscription. This march was massive with over 100,000 participants marching through Melbourne's city, making it one of the largest protests in Australian history. It was organised by a coalition of anti-war activists, politicians, trade union members, religious groups, academics and students who were united in their opposition to the war. It was a nonviolent and peaceful demonstration that reflected the broad opposition to the war. The air was alive with the sound of chants, with calls for peace and the rustle of banners swaying in the breeze. It felt like a river of people flowing through the city. Many of the crowd carried placards with slogans calling for peace or simply holding up their hand with the two-finger peace sign as I did. I felt good being a part of such a powerful peace movement.

The march was led by Jim Cairns – who was the deputy leader of the ALP, which was in opposition at the time – and Bob Hawke, who was the leader of the trade union movement, later to become Prime Minister. Due to mounting pressure in August 1971, Prime Minister Billy McMahon abolished conscription. In 1972, Prime Minister Gough Whitlam ended Australia's involvement in the Vietnam War.

At the end of 1970, my third year of studying law, I did very badly. I only passed one subject. I had more interest and excitement in my fashion agency, dedicating most of my time to it and very little to study. I was called before the selection committee at Monash and nervously stood in front of three professors. I told them about the agency business that I was running and explained that it had distracted me from my studies. I stated that if they let me repeat the year, I would give up my business.

They could see through me and explained that they believed I was more suited to business and not law, thus removing me from the law faculty. I was extremely embarrassed and upset. Most of my friends were still at university. Some also failed but switched courses or moved to universities interstate to continue their studies. There wasn't another course that interested me, so I sat at home trying to figure out how to enter the world of business.

Chapter 3

Over many weeks, I tossed and turned at night trying to decide what to do. With my beginnings of working in fashion at Mr Walker's store, the allure of Chesters Menswear where I was still working on Saturday mornings, the exhilaration of the Michelle Lucien agency and the increasing public interest in the rapidly changing styles of fashion, I knew that my future was to enter the fashion industry. It was the perfect fit for me and I did so with confidence. The year was 1971.

My older brother, Nick was working as a fashion agent for a young women's fashion label called Cumquat and had many contacts in the industry. The trendiest fashion store in Australia at that time was 'John and Merivale'. They sold fashion for both men and women and one of their best sellers was leather and suede pants. I thought these pants were great and as I hadn't seen them anywhere else; I decided to copy a pair and see if I could sell them to menswear stores. Nick knew of a small factory run by a lovely Greek couple that was making leather products, so I had a sample made. He financed me with $500 and for this, he became a full partner! I sold them to lots of menswear stores and felt there was also a demand for women, so I had another sample made and started selling them to women's stores as well. We called the label Ratso.

The demand for my leather range was growing and there was a buzz in the fashion industry about me. Leon, a friend of my brother, was involved in PR and arranged for me to meet a journalist from The Sun newspaper. They published an article about me on June 23rd, 1971, with the title, *The Suave Suede Man*. An excerpt from the article read as follows:

'Fashion design and the law may seem poles apart but not to Ian Swart, who studied law for three years before trying his hand at fashion design. His first foray was having a pair of suede trousers made. Ian had not been so confident about the success of this venture so he had the trousers made up in his own size so that at least he would have been able to wear them himself.

At first, Ian just designed men's suede trousers. Suede trousers for women were his next step. "Then I found that the shops were asking for skirts and shirts for the girls, so I branched into that field." His range now includes both suede and leather, hot pants, gauchos, boleros, vests, trousers, skirts, shirts and jackets. There is a good use of bright colour and patchwork effects. Ian's interest in fashion goes back several years to when he first started working in a men's wear store on a part-time basis. He still works in the store on Saturday mornings. "It's a good way to keep in touch with the retail market. A good designer should know what the buying public wants."'

As mentioned, my brother was working as an agent at Cumquat. Cumquat were making young female skirts, shirts, pants, etc. to sell to Sportsgirl, Myer, Sussan and smaller fashion boutiques. There were two partners involved and one wanted out, so Nick and I decided to purchase his share in 1972 and became partners with a wonderful man called Eli. We kept Ratso as a separate business in the same premises in Windsor where Cumquat was established.

I was still young and fresh in the business with lots to learn. I did learn in these early days how important building good relationships with people was. One relationship was with the owner of the Surf, Dive 'n' Ski stores. Ric was buying lots of jackets from me and became my biggest client. I delivered a large shipment of jackets to them one afternoon, expecting to be paid in seven days, which was our arrangement. Ric called me that same evening at about nine p.m. and told me to come straight in and collect my jackets as the business was going into liquidation the next morning. I drove in and retrieved them before the liquidators could confiscate them. A kind gesture, whilst not legal, but so generous as he didn't want me to lose out! I had established a good working relationship and a friendship with the owner of Surf, Dive 'n' Ski and from this experience realised that this was something I would always try to maintain in future dealings.

Chapter 4

I hadn't been overseas at this stage but had a desire to travel and see the world. Luckily, I had found an industry that gave me this opportunity. I started going to London and Paris, which were the fashion leaders, to source the latest trends and purchase samples that I would bring back to Australia so we could copy them for Cumquat and Ratso. This was common practice for people in the rag trade during the 70s. With Australia being in the southern hemisphere, we were a season behind and access to the fashion trends at the time was limited as there was no email, social media or online sales.

You didn't need to be a designer, just someone with a good eye to select samples overseas to copy. With my good eye, I was at one of the tanneries in Melbourne selecting leather skins for my jackets when I spotted a very soft pliable gorgeous leather. I was told that this was gloving leather made by Pittards in Yeovil, England, renowned to be the best gloving leather in the world. It felt strong enough whilst being thin to be used for jackets, especially suitable for women's jackets. I made a sample.

It was a hit and I made the most beautiful soft leather jackets out of gloving leather. It was doing so well that Pittards invited me to visit their factory in England. After being shown around their factory on a private tour, the directors invited me to have lunch in their private dining room. It was like a scene from a British movie. There I was in this high-ceilinged room with mahogany walls and a fire burning in the corner, silver service crockery and cutlery, top quality wines. Three directors in British suits joined me at the table and James this very chubby friendly in-house British chef with a handlebar moustache, wearing the full white chefs uniform, served me a delicious three-course lunch. I was receiving compliments about the quantity of leather I was purchasing and they confirmed that I was their first customer ever to transform their gloving leather into jackets. At the age of twenty-two, this lifted my enthusiasm and confidence for business.

On that same trip, I visited Harrods Department Store in London to look for samples for both Cumquat and Ratso. On the fourth floor was a trendy department called 'Way In'. I purchased lots of items to copy and left the store with both arms full of bags of clothing. I caught the underground rail heading back to the suburb of Richmond where I was staying. After several stops, I looked down to see where my manbag was. In it, of course, was my money, American Express card and my passport. It wasn't there! I panicked, got off at the next station, crossed platforms and headed back to Harrods' fourth floor. There it was, sitting on the counter where I had left it near the cash register about an hour earlier. Relief. I doubt that this would happen today.

On another trip to London, I met someone who imported Goulimine beads from Morocco. These were beautiful colourful beads up to about seven centimetres long that were used in traditional Berber jewellery. The beads were made up of colourful glass, sometimes metal and clay. I thought they were fabulous and bought a huge bag full, bringing them back to Australia. I had married in 1972 at the age of twenty-two and my wife Ester, a friend Louise and I would sit in the evening, threading leather through them to make necklaces and wristbands. We sold them to Sportsgirl but they sold slowly. About three years later, they became a huge trend with Australian surfies. I was too early with that one!

I was young and already showing signs of being a capable businessman. I was good at selling and my flare for product merchandising and colour was evident. I knew my big break would come but not yet as I had this burning desire to travel and explore the world's different cultures, food and history first. My adventure was about to begin.

MONASH UNIVERSITY
STUDENT IDENTITY CARD
ISSUED TO
NAME SWART IAN CONRAD
NUMBER 6945150
FAC. LAW   ISSUED 69
SIGNATURE
ECO / LAW

Michel Lucien Pty Ltd
Vic Agent
Ian Swart
tel: 50 2057

FASHION DESIGNING
WHOLESALERS
MANUFACTURERS
6 CAMPBELL STREET
SYDNEY Tel. 212 1168

DIRECTOR MANAGER
MICHEL MONSONEGO 32-4994

SALES MANAGER
GEORGES MOJICA

COMMONWEALTH OF AUSTRALIA
DEPARTMENT OF LABOUR AND NATIONAL SERVICE — National Service Registration Office
MELBOURNE 3000

Dear Sir,
This is to advise you that you have been granted indefinite deferment of your liability to render national service, and consequently, under present arrangements you will not be called up. Please keep your Certificate of Registration and this notice as evidence of your registration and deferment.

Yours faithfully,

W K Allen
Registrar

MR I C SWART
3 MOORAKYNE AV
MALVERN   VIC

Date 25/09/69
68 (REV.)—8/68

Registration Number 21332964

SUEDE LEATHER
Ratso

rag trade.
for a Syd
during a
decided t
facturing
that sue
very muc
maker, b
made pa
really i
manufac
respons
now flat
suede
The na
hardly
was a s
sion fo
better
Ratso

Ian Swart is a tender 21, although he looks older. He is one of the new breed of designers who miraculously get their fashion into high places with seemingly no help from a po

THINKING YOUNG
By CHRISTINA BUCKRIDGE

LAW student turned fashion designer Ian Swart shows some of his suede gear.

THE SUAVE SUEDE MAN

My Father's Business card,
South Africa, 1934

Grandfather Isadore, Bombay, 1936

My parents wedding, August 4, 1942

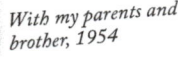

With my parents and
brother, 1954

Chapter 5

In the middle of 1974, Nick and I decided to sell the business as we both had the same desire to travel overseas indefinitely. Ester and I wanted to explore the world, its cultures, foods and history. We were young and had no commitments – we realised that this would be the only time in our lives that we could do this. We didn't sell the business for a huge amount but enough to get us over to Europe and sustain us for a few months. After a few months, we were enjoying our time away so much that we wanted to stay longer and realised we would need to work. We worked and remained on the road for two years. I would classify these as the most interesting and eye-opening years I have experienced.

It was hard in those times to plan travel and meet friends. Several of our friends were also travelling Europe at that time and the only way of communicating was via the American Express offices that would hold mail. So, we would write letters to each other. It was a difficult time for our parents as they never knew over the two years where we were and eagerly awaited a weekly letter from us or a phone call. International phone calls were very expensive so we would request reverse charges and keep the conversations brief.

Our adventure started in Greece after a seven-hour ferry ride to Mykonos where we were welcomed at the port by the resident pelican. Lots of ladies were at the port offering inexpensive rooms in their homes as there were no hotels on the island in those days. There were restaurants in the port that were homely and traditional. Octopus hung from the awnings, there was a limited menu, a jukebox for music and retsina wine.

One older lady shuffled over. She was small and slightly hunched over with a scarf covering her hair and long woollen socks under her skirt. Pointing her arthritic crooked finger at us, she offered us a room for $1.10. Ester and I looked at each other, not quite believing that a room could be so cheap. We followed our lady through the narrow winding streets. The houses were all white, many with colourful geraniums hanging from them. It was like walking through a maze. Apparently, it was purposely built like this to confuse the pirates who used to come and loot the islands. I don't know if it worked on the pirates, but it sure did on us as we spent hours and hours walking around on our first night trying to find our room. To our surprise, this cheap room was extremely clean and serviced but we had to share a bathroom. Breakfast was not included but our landlords were a gorgeous elderly couple who kept inviting us into their lounge for a Greek coffee.

Carl, a friend from home, was with us in Greece and he had a school friend David Agathos who was living on a beach called Paradise Beach, so we went to visit him and his girlfriend Kathy. Paradise Beach is on the other side of the island and is a beautiful beach with stunning sunsets. The only accommodation was tents on the sand or, like David and Kathy, living in a cave. We would go and visit them each day by bus followed by a twenty-minute walk. We brought fresh bread, tomatoes, cucumber, cheese and fruit for lunch as there were no restaurants. Today, Paradise Beach is lined with beach clubs, restaurants and bars offering music drinks and a lively party scene with sunbeds and umbrellas available for rent along the shore.

We were told that Santorini was a fascinating island to visit so after a couple of weeks of enjoying Mykonos, we caught a ferry there. On arrival, we could see a steep cliff face with a narrow winding track. The only way up was on the back of a pony – a very bumpy ride. We stayed several nights in the town of Thira and went for a day trip via a small ferry ride and quite a long hike to the still-active volcano, Nea Kameni. It was a live crater that was emitting large amounts of sulphuric gas. The island of Santorini had suffered great losses from this volcano; the last eruption recorded was in 1950.

We would go each day to Kamari Beach, which has black volcanic sand – too hot to walk on but very clean. There was a cute restaurant run by a big fat Greek lady offering simple and clean local food. Five dogs, six cats, a pelican, several donkeys and a few goats roamed the restaurant. Surrounding the beach and restaurant was a huge mountain rock, upon which the ruins of the ancient city of Thira lie. A stunning scene that lives in my memory.

Our third island was Ios and we felt we had reached Utopia. We found a two-roomed apartment for $1.80 per day belonging to a Greek lady from Athens. It was her home in the winter. A traditional Greek sideboard and cupboards, old photos, gold hanging lights and plastic-colourful tablecloths furnished the place. The village was very small with only one main street, the centre being only sixty metres from our apartment. There were no cars on the island.

The routine of our everyday day life was recorded in my diary as follows:

'We arise and have breakfast, which consists of the most beautiful Greek yogurt, honey and fresh bread and then buy our lunch to take with us. We catch the bus to the port and then walk about three-quarters of a mile over several hills to a beautifully secluded beach. By the time we get there, we are usually hungry, so we unpack our lunch consisting of fresh tomatoes, cucumber, olives, fetta cheese and delicious fresh bread, then sunbake and read the afternoon away. The evening we spend walking the port or village, listening to the Greek music that is playing on the jukeboxes, have dinner consisting of Souvlaki, meatballs and rice, moussaka, spaghetti, fresh fish or stuffed tomatoes. One of these meals costs $1.50 for two, including wine. We head to bed quite early. I don't remember ever having relaxed and read as much.'

No wonder we thought this was Utopia!

The island had few tourists as it was still basically undiscovered as a tourist destination. The only tourists we saw were a few Canadian and American hippies. They sat around the main street at the few outdoor cafes, singing, chatting and generally having fun, one café being reserved for the older men of the village.

After about six weeks on the Greek Islands, we returned to Athens and stayed with David and Kathy (from our time in Mykonos) for two weeks in his family home in Selianitika, which his parents had kept after moving to Australia.

During this time at David's home, war broke out. It was a strange feeling to be in a country on the brink of war. David, being Greek, was worried as he had cousins still living in Greece and was concerned that they would be called up. The Cypriot National Guard, supported by the Greek military junta, tried to overthrow the President of Cyprus to support unification with Greece. This caused tension between the Greek Cypriot and the minority Turkish Cypriot population. Turkey launched a military invasion and we were hearing radio announcements calling all Greek men to their stations. There were trains to Athens full of men reporting in and the trains to Patras, the nearby port, were full of tourists fleeing the country in a panic. All the streetlights were turned off.

The war finished within two weeks with a division of the island along ethnic grounds the northern part becoming the Turkish Republic of Northern Cyprus.

The Greek people were outraged by the Greek military junta. The junta collapsed and civilian democracy was returned to Greece. Smiling faces returned home and photos of the new Premier appeared in shop windows. Streetlights were switched back on and we felt safe to go out in the streets again.

We moved out of David's house and stayed in a small hotel at the base of the Plaka in Athens where we ventured to Syntagma Square, the most famous square in the centre of Athens. It was here we purchased a VW Combi van for $750. We had planned before leaving Australia to drive through Europe living in a van and had been told that Syntagma Square was where travellers bought and sold Combi vans. It was a 1968 green VW and had Australia written across the front in yellow. It was fully fitted out with cupboards, a stove, a double bed and curtains. This became our home for the next four months as we drove through much of Europe, staying overnight in campgrounds and visiting most of the famous tourist cities, towns and sights.

After four months on the road, money was running low, so we thought it was time to try and work. We were staying in a campground in Italy and saw an ad seeking hired help in the campground supermarket. We thought this could be fun – plus, it paid twenty-three dollars per week and free food. We started work bright and early and enthusiastically rearranged the entire place. After five hours, we were totally exhausted but kept working. We were proud of our effort and thought it would be appreciated but towards the end of the day, our gentle Italian employer became very angry and outraged at us for interfering and changing what he felt was his perfectly set up supermarket. He didn't appreciate our product merchandising skills. He threw us out. We were sacked on the spot for being too officious and he told us not to return. We happily departed that campground, celebrating that night with a bottle of wine!

Chapter 6

Having Dutch parents, I thought it would be great to visit and seek employment in Holland, so we ventured to Amsterdam. I was excited to converse in Dutch, which I had never really spoken before except for a few odd words but as my parents always spoke Dutch at home to each other and their friends, I could fully understand it. The Dutch speak excellent English and to my disappointment, when I spoke to them in Dutch, they could hear me struggling so they would reply in English.

Without citizenship or a work permit, I went from agency to agency to no avail. Finally, I went to a student employment agency. The employee commented, 'With a name like Yan Zwart, no problem,' so I got a job in an old people's home as a kitchenhand, preparing the coffee and tea trays and washing the dishes. I worked there for about three months. The beauty for me was that the workers, three middle-aged ladies, didn't speak English so I could practice my Dutch conversation. Ester got a job as a waitress in a brown uniform at the Hilton Hotel coffee shop by telling them her husband was Dutch. She kept forgetting to bring my Dutch papers, which, of course, didn't exist.

As it was the beginning of winter, sleeping in our van was freezing. It was raining constantly and the sound of it pounding onto the van's tin roof kept us awake. We would step outside in the morning into mud and slush. As there were not many tourists in winter, we moved into a hotel at a cheap weekly rate and lived there for the entire time. It was terrific living under a roof again, having hot showers and a toilet close by. The hotel kitchen was closed so we were able to use it to cook our meals, which we did most nights. I was fortunate that each morning, I could take a fifteen-minute walk to work through Vondelpark, which is Amsterdam's largest and most picturesque park. It is one of Amsterdam's favourite spots for a stroll, a bike ride along its pathways, sports, a picnic, eating at some of its cafes or simply relaxing and reading a book.

My brother, cousin and their wives joined us and moved into the same hotel, so we had a fun time. I arranged for my sister-in-law Ricci to work with me in the kitchen. Virtually every night after dinner, we would go to the Melkweg or the Paradiso.

The Melkweg was something that didn't exist and still doesn't anywhere in the world. Downstairs was a market that sold hippie clothes, beads, drug paraphernalia and more. There were tables selling all types of marijuana or hashish from Nepal, Afghanistan, India and Morocco.

On the ground floor was a restaurant and a tearoom that had a tented ceiling where you would sit on cushions, drink exotic teas and eat hash cake or cookies.

On the first floor was quite a large room where local bands would play most nights or a DJ would be playing music so we could dance the night away. Next to that was a small movie theatre where you also sat on cushions and laughed through old silent movies whilst very stoned. The Paradiso was more of a music venue so when good bands were playing, we would venture there.

The law in the Netherlands at that time allowed people to sell and smoke cannabis at the Melkweg and Paradiso but not in the streets. It was illegal to buy, sell or smoke in the street. From memory, the Melkweg was closed on Monday nights. One Monday night, we felt like a smoke but didn't have any so Nick and I ventured down to the street where the Melkweg was to do a deal. We found a dealer and as we were doing the transaction, a police car pulled up.

The dealer threw his stash away and the police told us, 'Hands up and stand against the wall.'

I have never stood straighter or taller! They frisked us and asked why we were buying hashish when it was illegal. We put on the ignorant tourist act and explained that we thought we should try some and were under the impression that it was legal in Amsterdam. They let us go but took the dealer with them. We made sure from then on only to buy in the Melkweg. We did go back later to see if we could find the hash that the dealer threw but to no avail. Guess someone else got lucky before we returned!

My command of the Dutch language improved greatly from working in the kitchen and on the many trips to Amsterdam since, I always try to speak in Dutch. I loved Amsterdam from the moment we got there. Listening to Dutch being spoken around me was a buzz as I had only ever heard it in my home or my grandparents' place. The Dutch food I had grown up with was served everywhere and the quaintness of Amsterdam with its narrow streets and canal network somehow gave me a feeling of belonging. Since that time, I have always made an effort to include Amsterdam whenever I visit Europe even if it is only for a couple of days. Each time, I make a beeline to my favourite food places I discovered when we lived there: a sandwich shop Van Dobben's at Rembrandts Plein, my favourite 'frite with mayonaise' (French fry) stall off the Kalverstraat, the best Herring stand on the Leidseplein, poffertjes (Dutch mini pancakes) on Roken, Rookewurst (Dutch smoked sausage) from the Hamer Store, the traditional Dutch restaurant near the Dam Square that has been there since the 1600s and, naturally, the various coffee shops serving hashish unique to the city.

Though my Dutch had improved, it wasn't always perfect. On one of my visits to Amsterdam in the early 1980s, between my marriages, I met an attractive girl and tried my hand in Dutch to woo her over. It must be remembered that my parents emigrated to Australia in the 1930s, so their Dutch was old-fashioned. When she asked me how I got to Holland from Australia, I replied, 'By a *vliegmachine*,' which literally translates to a 'flying machine' – a word not used in Holland since before the Second World War. She looked at me in amazement, like I was an alien from outer space and quickly found an excuse to leave me standing at the bar, glass in hand, wondering where I went wrong. I since found out that the correct word for an aeroplane is 'vliegtuig'.

My Dutch did improve, and I concentrated on avoiding using old-fashioned words. On a later visit, I purchased clothing and a pair of shoes from a department store, speaking only in Dutch. After the purchase, the salesperson asked me how long I had been living out of Holland, believing me to be a Dutchman with a slight foreign accent. That made me feel proud!

Chapter 7

Together with Nick and his first wife Ricci, Ester and I flew from Holland to Morocco in December of 1974 for a two-week journey. We assumed that it would be warm as it was North Africa, but it was winter and freezing and as we only packed our summer clothes, we basically wore the same winter Amsterdam clothes every day.

It was another exotic destination and we have wonderful memories of Fez and Marrakesh particularly. Marrakesh is a fairytale city. It is an ancient walled city with the high Atlas Mountains visible in the distance. The marketplace at Djemaa el-Fna is alive in the evenings with jugglers, dancers, magicians, storytellers, snake charmers and music. They roll in food carts with exotic Moroccan meals and delicacies. It's a very exciting and unique vibe sitting at the food carts and watching the activity surrounding you. (My wife Gina and I revisited Marrakesh in July 2018 with our friends David and Jo Samad from New York who are also in the rug business. The vibe in Marrakesh and Fez was very similar to how it was in 1974.)

From Marrakesh, we took a bus to the Atlas Mountains, a mountain range that stretches across Morocco. It was the day before Eid al-Adha, a celebration to mark the end of the Hajj pilgrimage and to honour the prophet, Abraham. Abraham was instructed to sacrifice his son; however, God replaced this with a sheep and this tradition has continued. As the following day was the sacrificial day there were live sheep tied to the roof of the bus. The four of us shared a room and were kept up all night by the sound of the sheep, which the locals had taken into their bedrooms for the night. We couldn't stop laughing when in the morning we saw the man in the room next to us leave with his sheep under his arm.

We decided not to take the bus back down to Marrakesh but hired a driver to take us through the sights of the Atlas Mountains, where we saw breathtaking rugged landscapes, snow-capped peaks and traditional Berber villages where we saw the sheep being sacrificed or roasting on the spit.

The roads were winding, narrow and icy. Nick sat in the front seat next to the driver the three of us sat in the back. As we were coming down the mountain slope heading back to Marrakesh, I could see through the rear vision mirror that the driver was dosing off. I told Nick so he started hitting him on the arm to keep him awake and we made him stop several times for coffee. That was quite a hair-raising experience!

In Marrakesh, we wandered into beautiful exotic old rug stores that served tea on arrival. We loved the Berber-style rugs that were adorning the walls and stacks. There was a certain smell from the wool in the stores, a smell that I would notice permeating all rug stores and warehouses ever since and even in my own stores, particularly noticeable when I haven't entered the stores for several days. There were basically two styles of Berber rugs: the simpler, plush, soft-feeling cream-coloured rugs and the very colourful, flat-piled, tribal-looking pieces mainly adorned with a red background.

Our father had recently opened his Persian rug shop in Toorak Rd South Yarra. In one of the beautiful rug stores in Marrakesh, Nick and I looked at each other and at the same time, we clicked on the idea that we should buy some of these colourful Berber rugs for our father to sell in his new Persian carpet shop. So we bargained heavily – as you always do in Morocco and as is expected of you – purchased several and shipped them home. He hated them and I don't even think he made any effort to sell them. They were handed back to us when we eventually arrived home. We kept some and sold the balance to our friends. The outcome was not what I had expected but it was my first foray into rug buying and I enjoyed the thrill of selecting, bargaining and purchasing them.

Chapter 8

After returning from Morocco to Amsterdam, we thought it was time to move on so Ester and I decided that London would be a great spot to work and live for a time. As my mother had been born in London, I had pre-arranged a work permit.

I wrote to my parents soon after arriving in London and mentioned to them that I had visited most of the Persian rug stores in both Amsterdam and London and from what I could ascertain, they had a much wider variety and more interesting carpets than I had seen in Australia. I sent my father photographs of what I thought were beautiful rugs. He never really commented but probably disliked my choice as he did with the Moroccan rugs. My interest in rugs was obviously growing!

We rented a house with friends in Hampstead in a great position opposite Hampstead Heath, a beautiful massive rambling and hilly park covering 320 hectares with ponds, playgrounds, training tracks, ancient woodlands and large grassy areas. Our home was a four-storey terrace house, and we rented the top two floors. Downstairs lived an elderly couple, Mr and Mrs Corcoran, who were our landlords. They hadn't opened their windows in years and their place and their bodies had this putrid stale stench. I think they may have bathed once a year.

In the basement, they had stored lots of furniture and allowed us to take up whatever we wished, so we ended up with a fully furnished apartment. There weren't any beds so Mrs Corcoran said she would buy us some. I took her in my van to a bed store and she purchased new beds for us. I could hardly breathe in the van with the stale stench that was coming off her! They often fought and we could hear lots of yelling going on. One time, Mrs Corcoran knocked on our door and told me that Mr Corcoran had thrown her out of the apartment. I went downstairs with her and knocked on the door. He answered very sweetly and said, 'Dear, what are you doing outside in the cold? Please do come in.'

I applied and got a job at Jean Machine on Kings Road, Chelsea. I was excited to be in the fashion field again, especially after washing dishes for several months. Each day I would get to the bus stop at Hampstead Heath (the start of the line), go upstairs, grab the front seat and off it would go, giving me a tour of London all the way to Chelsea. The bus would pass through Swiss Cottage, Regents Park, the British Museum, Trafalgar Square, Leicester Square, Piccadilly Circus, Buckingham Palace and Knightsbridge, ending at Sloan Square where I had a short walk up Kings Road to the store.

I knew I had more potential than being a salesman without a senior role, so after two weeks I went to see management and asked for a meeting with the HR manager. I told him I had previously run a fashion business in Australia and that I had more to offer than just being a salesman and needed more responsibility. His first reaction was that I was too young but I was convincing, and he promoted me to manager. It was an incredible time. To earn extra money, Ester and I did the shortening of jeans at home, charging sixty pence per pair. I would pin them up at the store, mark them with chalk at home and Ester would machine them on a borrowed sewing machine.

Jean Machine had nine shops just on Kings Rd, Chelsea alone where I worked, plus thirteen others spread over London. It was the time of the jean explosion. People came from all corners of the globe to buy jeans in London. One time, a bus of Iranians pulled up outside the store and we sold them 300 pairs of jeans in one go. Barbara Streisand, Jane Asher (who was Paul McCartney's girlfriend), Tony Curtis and Gene Wilder all came to the store during my time and I was fortunate to speak to them all. When Tony Curtis came in, I was serving him when a young junior working there went up to him and said, 'Hello, Mr Curtis.' His reply was, 'Hello, Martin. How are you?' Tony was a friend of Martin's father, so I let him take over the sale.

I had my own taste of celebrity status when I was standing outside the jean store and a couple walked past wearing Jag denim, an Australian label. Trying to be smart, I called out, 'Oh, a little bit of Australia.' They looked me straight in the eye and replied, 'You must be Ian Swart.' I almost fell over. Was I that famous? Turns out that they were friends of my brother Nick and had been told that I was working in a jeans shop in London.

After five months of enjoying and working in London, we had saved money and decided to get on the road again so we sold the camper van outside Australia House in Earls Court. Earls Court was where most Australians stayed and outside Australia House was where camper vans were bought and sold as in Syntagma Square in Athens. We planned to head back to the Greek Islands for another summer. With our friends Len and Rhonda from Australia, we bought a 1964 Mk2 Jaguar for ninety pounds. This was equivalent to three weeks' rent of our Hampstead Heath apartment, so it was a bargain. Even better, I sold the silver Jaguar motif that was mounted on the bonnet for thirty-five pounds. We bought two-man tents, mess kits and a small portable stove and off we headed, living in our tents on camping grounds.

This journey took us through the southern part of France to visit a couple Len had met earlier in his travels. We stayed with them for eight days in a beautiful old medieval French village called Lourmarin. It is a picturesque Provence town nestled amongst rolling hills and olive groves, with cobblestoned streets and buildings adorned with colourful shutters, the 15th Century Renaissance castle towering over the village. We enjoyed walking, visiting the local market, and eating beautiful French sticks, local cheese and drinking local wine. Our host, Michael, cooked us delicious French meals each night.

We drove on through the Riviera, Italy and into Yugoslavia. Yugoslavia at that time was a communist country under the strict rule of Tito. It has since been divided into seven countries: Croatia, Serbia, Slovenia, Montenegro, Macedonia, Bosnia and Herzegovina. Driving down the coast, we found the people to be quite unfriendly and repressed; however, once we drove inland and around Albania, it all changed. The people were welcoming and waved as we drove passed. Whenever we stopped, kids would surround the car and stare at us through the windows. The countryside was extremely green and mountainous and the people on the land wore colourful traditional gypsy outfits and many travelled around by horse and cart, the horses bridle also being colourful. In each village, there was a Turkish quarter, as the Turks once ruled this area, and visiting the traditional Turkish markets gave us a feeling of excitement like we had felt in Morocco. Most people here seemed happy under Tito's rule compared to those further north.

When we arrived in Greece, we stopped at a campground in the north. The weather changed. It started raining heavier than I had ever seen and didn't seem to stop. Over the water, we could see cyclones in the distance. Our tents were soaking so we packed up and went to a nearby hotel. The rain did not stop so we decided it was time to move on. Len went to get the car, bringing it closer to our room. He drove about twenty metres straight into a tree. The brakes had failed so we were stranded in the floods. A couple of days later, our car was repaired and we headed to Athens.

On arrival in Athens, we went to a couple of car yards to try and sell the car. Fortunately, the second yard we went to showed interest and we sold him the car for the same amount that we had paid in London so the trip through Europe only cost us petrol, new brakes and a radiator hose. Beautiful weather was once again in front of us and for our second summer we spent six weeks exploring more of the Greek islands.

Chapter 9

We were contemplating where to go next and the idea of visiting Israel, the land of our forefathers, was most interesting and inviting. The history of Israel – which both of us had been taught in Jewish Sunday school – photos we had seen of the old city of Jerusalem and Bethlehem, the modernisation of Tel Aviv, the vast desert areas and volunteering on a kibbutz, which we had learnt about and knew that you could stay for free, made the decision for us. We caught a short flight from Athens to Israel where we toured this fascinating historic biblical land for a month. It was a very different feeling to be in a country where a large majority of the residents were Jewish. After our touring, we volunteered on a kibbutz called Bar'am where we remained for a few months.

A kibbutz is a community living together with a strong sense of socialism and shared ownership of the property. They were founded on the principles of economic and social equality and strived for self-sufficiency. Many had their own factories, schools and health services. Members worked together to cultivate the land, raise livestock and manage various agricultural enterprises. They lived in communal housing, typically being small apartments or houses usually arranged around a central dining hall and social spaces. The kibbutz had a system of collective child rearing, with children living in separate children's houses. The kibbutz took care of the children's education and after school, the children would spend time with their parents.

It was very popular for tourists from all over Europe, Australia and America to volunteer and work on a kibbutz. The kibbutz welcomed volunteers to assist with the work needed. Bar'am was mainly involved in agriculture so the volunteers were given work during the day from picking oranges and apples, cleaning chickens and helping in the kitchen to setting the tables, etc.

Life for volunteers was free as board and food were provided. Most of the volunteers weren't Jewish so Ester and I were often asked to remain and become members. Some of the members were very pushy, which probably put us off staying.

Bar'am was only three-quarters of a kilometre from the Lebanese border and therefore in an area of potential terrorist attacks. It was surrounded by barbed wire with guard dogs chained at various points around the fence. There were watchtowers spread evenly and at night a patrol jeep fitted with a searchlight and machine gun drove continuously around. The kibbutzniks all carried sub-machineguns whether it be to the dining room or the swimming pool. It was amazing that after a few days of living on this Kibbutz, we didn't notice this anymore.

What brought to light the reason for all this security was the day in which we experienced a manoeuvre that lasted five hours. They staged a mock attack, the reason being that if the kibbutz was attacked it would take at least an hour for the army to arrive, so they needed to protect themselves. We were confined to our quarters, but I snuck out to try and capture the action on film. There were explosions going off in the kibbutz, the children were rushed to the bunkers, and kibbutzniks ran with their guns to their posts and began shooting into the woods as a helicopter swooped overhead. This manoeuvre made me realise how tough it was to be an Israeli with the continual threat of the Arab neighbours attacking over the borders as they had done recently in the 1973 Yom Kippur War and the 1967 Six-day War. This was my experience of seeing first-hand what happens if attacked. No question it was scary and the Israelis needed to be continually on alert as this was an attack that could happen at any time. I was very glad not to experience the real thing.

Kibbutz life in the 1970s retained many of its core principles but also faced economic changes as Israel adopted new technologies in their agricultural and industrial practices. By the 1980s, due to changes in lifestyle, kibbutz numbers were reducing. In response many introduced various forms of privatisation, moving away from the original socialistic model to try and encourage members to stay.

Kibbutzim today are quite different as now they are engaged in industries including technology, manufacturing, tourism and services as well as still being involved in agriculture. Education is still conducted in the kibbutz but the practice of collective child-rearing has almost disappeared with most kibbutzim now emphasising family units living a more traditional family life as one unit.

The Corcoran's our landlords in London

Chapter 10

We loved our time in Israel but the yearn to travel on and experience different cultures was strong, so we decided to move on. We had heard from many travellers, mainly in Israel and Greece, that travelling overland through Asia on the Hippie Trail was an unbelievable experience so for our next journey, we flew to Istanbul where the infamous Hippie Trail started.

Lots of young tourists, mainly hippies, were doing the overland trip on a bus called 'The Magic Bus' that started in London and went overland to Nepal, the longest bus journey in the world but we decided to do it our way. It was known to be a fascinating journey as one got to encounter various cultures, lifestyles, beliefs and customs, steeped with long history. Most importantly at that time, it was peaceful throughout the entire region. India was the main destination for hippies in the 1970s as India had a reputation for adventure, spiritual enlightenment, meditation practises, yoga, an alternative lifestyle, a lenient attitude to drug taking and was extremely budget-friendly.

Our first Asian city was Istanbul, which gave us an introduction to what was to come. The streets were dirty and a sweet and pungent smell filled the air. The people dressed in Asian-style clothing. The markets – or souks, as they are called – had more people in them than I had ever seen. Men were smoking shisha pipes and carpet stores were in abundance with huge stacks of carpet styles that I had not seen before. They had unique patterns, motifs and colours that were vastly different to the Persian carpets that were familiar to me and also to those I had seen and purchased in Morocco. I kept thinking about my father, wanting to let him know that there was a whole world of carpets out there that he was unaware of but after the reaction we got from the Moroccan purchase, I stayed quiet.

The skyline was filled with tall minarets of the many mosques in Istanbul, the stunning Blue Mosque being the most famous. It is a beautiful Byzantine and Islamic architectural structure with 20,000 blue tiles adorning the interior and blue-painted walls. The floor is covered with traditional rugs in layers complementing the stunning interior design. They don't ever remove them but as they begin to wear out, a new layer is added. The rugs serve as a comfortable surface for worshipers to kneel and pray on.

Another stunning structure in Istanbul is one of the world's largest surviving palaces, Top Kapi Palace, which was built as early as 1460. It blew me away as I couldn't believe the beauty and style of this stunning example of Ottoman architecture. The palace is a maze of courtyards, gardens and buildings plus a wing that held the emperor's Harem. The museum section has the world's largest collection of Ottoman Empire artefacts and jewels. This was our first introduction to the Asian history of riches, many of which were to follow.

We made our way to the Pudding Shop in the Sultanahmet area of Istanbul, which was the meeting place of hippies in the 1970s. It had a laid-back atmosphere and communal seating – and it was our first introduction to Turkish cuisine. It had a variety of vegetarian options: stews of eggplant tomatoes, fresh vegetables and lentil soups. Lamb and chicken kebabs were available and, as the name suggests, Turkish puddings, The most popular was 'iskele tatlisi' (pudding with cinnamon).

The Pudding Shop was like an information hub. Travellers from around the world shared experiences. Those who were returning to Europe after their overland trip plus, those who began their journey in Australia, were sharing stories with those beginning their overland journey heading East with advice as to where to visit. We made new friends as we heard about the different cultures and traditions that we would encounter as you traversed through the various countries. There was a noticeboard for those who were looking for others to travel overland with and people with cars or vans offering rides to share the costs. We caught a ride in a beautifully fitted out van with an English couple by sharing the petrol cost. Eastern Turkey was quite primitive and can be dangerous, so we teamed up with two other vans and drove in a convoy for five days. Twice we had stones thrown at us from the side of the road. The villages were swarming with impoverished barefooted children and swarms of men with hardly a female to be seen, as they were basically confined to their homes. If we did see a woman, she would be wearing the full hijab whilst the men wore Western clothes. Wherever we stopped, kids would surround the van and whether they were five or sixteen years old, they would ask us for cigarettes.

Most of the drive was desert. There were beautiful sights, however, and as we got closer to Iran, we saw a magnificent array of colours in the undulating countryside and snow-capped mountains both left and right of us. We drove very near Mount Ararat, which was an incredible, treacherous-looking black mountain, standing 5,000 metres high.

Chapter 11

When we crossed the border into Iran, everything changed. The roads became wider and in good repair, the towns and villages had modern buildings, lots of construction was going on and the children were wearing neat school uniforms on their way to modern-looking schools. The men wore Western clothes, many in jeans and jean jackets. The women also wore Western clothes with a fine traditional veil, in various patterns and designs to match their clothes, over their heads and down to their ankles. It was a very attractive look. This was the time when the Shah was in power, and his aim was for Iran to follow Western values, economic prosperity and modernisation. In contrast, Iran is now a very different country under strict religious leadership.

We parted with our friends in the city of Tabriz after covering 1900 kilometres as they were heading in a different direction. We caught an overnight train to Tehran and on arrival, we found it to be noisy, crowded, dirty and the traffic extremely chaotic. We wanted to move on as quickly as possible, so we caught a taxi from the station straight to the Afghan embassy, expecting to wait at least forty-eight hours for the visa, as this is what fellow travellers had told us. Luck was with us and we were given a visa after only waiting thirty minutes. Leaving the embassy, we found it impossible to find a taxi but fortunately, a friendly Iranian couple gave us a lift back to the station where, after a period of frustration, we found a hotel nearby.

Next day we caught a train to Mashhad. Straight from the railway station, we sped by taxi to the bus depot where we were just in time to catch the bus to Taybad. Arriving four hours later and totally exhausted, we searched for a hotel room. We were the only tourists in town and there were only two hotels. Even though we were quite used to roughing it, they were absolutely disgusting so we hitched a ride to the border fifteen kilometres away. A car stopped and offered us a ride for a small fee. This ride was hilarious as we realised that our driver was in the middle of his driving lesson and the teacher next to him had control of the pedals.

Arriving at the border, we had no problem with the Iranian customs and once through, we were told that the Afghan border was six kilometres away through desert land. There were two young long-haired Norwegians at customs travelling through Asia in a camper van so they kindly gave us a lift to the Afghan border, arriving just in time as it was about to close. It was like a scene in a movie. We were filling in complex formalities, darkness was approaching and we had no idea what lay ahead. We didn't realise that Herat was 120 kilometres away and there were no more buses. The Norwegians saved us again by driving us all the way to Herat, arriving at night, thoroughly exhausted.

Travelling through Iran, we saw lots of beautiful Persian rugs in stores or hanging from balconies, on hotel floors and thrown on the roads. They allowed cars, trucks, people, camels to traipse over them, with the sun shining so that they would be given an antique used look. I admired the beautiful variety and once again thought about my father not knowing that one day rugs would be my world.

Chapter 12

Arriving in Herat at night, we immediately felt a good vibe. Driving through this ancient town in the dark, with only a spattering of streetlights felt comfortable. We were so tired after such a long day of travel that we collapsed into bed but the anticipation of exploring Herat the next day kept my mind going and I struggled to fall asleep. Our hotel was clean, the people were friendly and the food was delicious. In the morning, we walked out of the hotel excited to explore this ancient city that travellers we met at the Pudding Shop all raved about. The first thing we encountered were two ladies walking past us in full burkas and one said in clear English, 'Welcome to Afghanistan.'

It gave us a warm and fuzzy feeling. Herat was a beautiful and exotic tranquil city that was set in a time warp. It had amazing old bazaars and beautiful historic sights. Hashish was available everywhere. We sat in cafés where the owner would have a huge slab of hash, which he would cut up in slabs about the size of a fist and charge you twenty dollars. People sat around smoking from large clay pipes called chillums. After a few puffs of this potent hash, it was hard to get back up so from memory, we spent most of our time in Herat sitting in these cafés being very stoned.

Once more, we came across rug stores, which were vibrant marketplaces. The rugs were different again as they were characterised by bold geometric patterns and vibrant colour palettes, mainly deep red, blue and earth tones with different geometric designs of hexagons, octagons and tribal symbols. They were thick and solid and instantly became my favourite rugs. There were also beautiful geometric pastel-coloured kelims (flat pile rugs). I had never seen these in Australia and once again had my father in my thoughts.

After a few delightful days in magical Herat, we bused through the countryside via Kandahar to Kabul. We rode on an old windowless rickety bus on a very bumpy road for fourteen hours packed with passengers dressed in traditional Afghan attire. Most of the men wore turbans and loose-fitting shalwar kameez, the women in traditional Afghan embroidered dresses or fully covered in a black hijab. The landscape was breathtaking, from mountain ranges to vast deserts and picturesque valleys. As we drove through small villages, we would pass vibrant markets, traditional bazaars and streets bustling with locals walking, driving, on donkeys or on the occasional camel.

In Kabul, all the action was around Chicken Street where it seemed that some enterprising Afghans had embraced the hippie culture by creating a cosmopolitan atmosphere in tea houses, offering exotic teas and a huge variety of hashish. Backgammon was the game of choice and the sound of The Eagles, Fleetwood Mac or Pink Floyd played in the background. There were small hotels that were extremely clean, having beautiful garden settings and room service all for one dollar per night. Lots of restaurants were in the area, a good three-course meal costing us $1.80 for two. There was a large chicken market (hence the name) that also sold food, local crafts and clothing.

We shopped in the market and from here, we changed our everyday look as the clothing on offer suited the warmer climate and set the frame of hippie-style clothing. Ester bought peasant-style loose-fitting blouses and long flowing skirts in vibrant colours with embroidery and mirror work. I purchased cotton or linen flowing shirts, vests, flowing bell-bottom cotton pants and small Afghan hats. We both bought handmade leather sandals. We now felt very much a part of the journey we were on.

I really enjoyed the Afghan food and found there was a larger variety than the staple diet of kebab and rice offered in Iran. Afghan cuisine is a delightful fusion of flavours. One iconic dish is 'Kabuli pulao', a rice dish featuring lamb or beef, raisins, carrots and spices. 'Mantu' are delicate dumplings filled with spiced minced meat usually served with yogurt and mint. As in Iran and Turkey, chicken and beef kebabs served with rice are a staple. The ancient way of making Tandoor bread fascinated me. Baked in a clay oven, which was dug into the ground, the dough would be shaped into flattened rounds then slapped into the inner walls of the preheated oven where it would stick to the walls, baking rapidly, and when cooked to perfection, it would be removed with long tandoor tongs.

I couldn't help but to be drawn to the many rug stores that were dotted around the area we were residing in. They were of similar patterns to the ones I had seen in Herat but as it was a much larger city, the variety was greater with some stunning pieces. I would go each day for a walk to rummage through their pieces. Ester, not as interested, would stay at our hotel. These stores were mostly family-owned businesses passed through generations. Most were small, more like stalls with stacks of rugs folded and pressed against the walls. There were saddlebags, camel bags and camel and donkey trappings for sale. The strong smell of camel and horses permeated out into the streets. Afghan tents, known as a 'yurt', were made of a wooden framework covered with woven textiles and as a doorway, they would have a rug known as a Hatchlu. The stores were selling these and they became my favourite rug, both in colour and design. I didn't purchase one on this trip but was able to purchase one on one of my later buying trips. I still treasure this rug and it sits prominently on the floor of my study at home.

We experienced something quite special on the outskirts of Kabul: a game of Buzkashi. Buzkashi, literally meaning 'dragging of a goat', is an ancient sport played in Afghanistan that involves riders on horseback competing to grab a goat carcass and move it towards and across the goal line whilst navigating through opposing riders. There are two teams of about ten horsemen, and it is often referred to as a primitive form of

Polo. The game we saw was in a large open field and along the edge were loads of decorated Afghan trucks with locals all on the roofs of the trucks while the game progressed. It was very rough and exciting to watch.

We kept bumping into other travellers that we had met in Greece and Turkey and made friendships never feeling that we were on our own. We loved our time in Herat and Kabul but decided to move on and make our way to India as this was the favourite place of most travellers.

From Kabul, we travelled through the Kabul Gorge to Jalalabad on our way to Pakistan. Kabul is situated in a narrow valley and is one of the highest capital cities in the world. The gorge is part of the Kabul River Valley and is a dramatic drive through the Hindu Kush Mountains. The two-lane highway was only completed in 1969 and driving along it was like a visual feast as we came across historical sights, arid stretches and lush green areas. There were towering mountain cliffs rising dramatically on either side of the narrow highway, deep valleys and for most of the way, the Kabul River flowed alongside or below the road.

The road took us to the border of Pakistan and the beginning of the drive through the Khyber Pass, one of the original routes of the Silk Road that took us down to the city of Peshawar. The drive was challenging, breathtaking and sometimes treacherous as we bussed along a narrow winding road with lots of twists and turns as it snaked its way through steep cliffs and rocky terrain. We saw a landscape dotted with centuries-old forts, rugged mountains and glimpses of local life in villages dotted along the route. Tunnels had been bored through the mountains to ease the passage. Rudyard Kipling described it as 'a sword cut through a mountain'.

Driving through the Kabul Gorge and the Khyber Pass was by far the most dramatic and sensory drive I have ever been on.

We arrived in Peshawar at evening time. This was a city of contrasts, blending ancient traditions with modern developments. It had a lovely historic old city with narrow alleyways and a melting pot between Pakistan and Afghanistan with the traditions of both cultures. However, it lacked the inviting peaceful vibe of the places we had explored throughout Afghanistan due to a large military presence, so we found a small hotel and the next day moved on.

Chapter 13

Pakistan had the worst reputation amongst overland travellers of any country in Asia. It was under strict military rule and was not conducive to leisurely travel as compared to other countries in the region. It had very strict laws governing drug use, possession, alternative lifestyles and unconventional clothing. We therefore trained through as quickly as possible, hoping all the way that we wouldn't be stopped by any authorities, and made sure that we didn't have any drugs in our possession. I diarised on October 27, 1975, that 'when you travel by train through Pakistan, your mind is blown away by an endless procession of beggars, musicians and hawkers'.

The border between Pakistan and India was stunning with magnificent gardens on both sides of the border and an expanse of no man's land between. Only foreigners were allowed to cross this border because although both countries gained independence from Britain in 1948, there was still a permanent state of near war. Both countries' borders were heavily guarded and there was no transport of any kind. However, there were hundreds of Pakistani men in red shirts carrying boxes on their heads from Pakistan halfway through no man's land where they were met by hundreds of Indian men in blue shirts transporting the boxes across to India. We walked across no man's land to the Indian border and were greeted by a handsome tall Sikh soldier wearing a turban, a large twirling moustache, a net concealing his beard and an immaculate military outfit. He welcomed us to 'Mother India'. There was a poorly stencilled sign on plain wood stating, 'Welcome to India,' and immediately, a tremendous feeling of euphoria came over me.

Thirty kilometres from the border was our first taste of India, the city of Amritsar. This was an eye-opener, our first introduction to the wonderful land that we were about to experience. The city streets were alive with the sights and sounds of daily life. Thousands of people were walking, driving, in taxis, in cars, on tuk-tuks, bicycles and even riding elephants. It is the hub of the Sikh heritage where most of the men wear the traditional Sikh turban and a Kurta, which is a long tunic-like loose-fitting shirt usually made of cotton. The women wear a long tunic top, paired with loose-fitting trousers and a matching scarf or shawl draped stylishly over their head or around the neck. They adorn themselves with lots of jewellery – dangling earrings, chokers and lots of bangles. The smell of Punjabi cuisine filled the air. We saw a mixture of traditional Indian buildings interlaced with public buildings designed during the time of the British rule. In the centre was the Golden Temple, one of the most revered and iconic religious sites in India. It is a two-storey building built of marble and overlaid with gold leaf. It stands in the centre of a pool and houses the Guru Granth Sahib, the central religious scripture of Sikhism. Tourists and pilgrims from all over the world visit as it has one of the largest free kitchens in the world, serving free meals twenty-four hours per day to all, regardless of their background or social status, reflecting the Sikh principles of selfless service (seva) and equality. The food is served in an atmosphere of complete silence and devotion. At the main temple, Sikh music and hymns could be heard throughout the day. We were moved by the Golden Temple and spent two days near and around this magnificent building, its surrounds and activity, never quite game enough to try the free food.

We then took a fourteen-hour scary bus trip up the mountains to Srinagar Kashmir on a potholed narrow road just wide enough for buses to pass each other. There was a sheer drop on one side and the driver was racing up fearlessly. Ester cried for the entire drive and I made out that there was nothing to worry about but inside, I was really shitting myself with the fear that we would topple over the edge.

Srinagar is a beautiful place with a civilisation that lives and works on the lakes together. It is set amongst mountains and numerous canals joining several lakes. There are islands with gardens on them, floating gardens and lilies growing out of the water. Dal Lake is the largest lake and there are houseboats dotted along the shore.

Renting a houseboat for about a week was wonderful. The wooden houseboats are traditional and decorated in a Colonial style quite lavishly. We paid US$4.50 per day for two bedrooms, a loungeroom, a dining room and a bathroom. This included three servants, three meals a day, afternoon tea, supper tea and they also placed a hot water bottle in our bed as the nights were cool. The view of the mountains surrounding the lake was spectacular. It was a most relaxing and serene place to visit.

Every day, small boats called Shikaras, which were like Italian gondolas, would come up to the houseboat with fresh produce and handicrafts, the most famous of which is paper mâché. Paper mâché has been made in Kashmir since the fifteenth century and is done by layering strips of paper over a mould and then intricately decorating it with fine brushwork recreating elaborate traditional motifs. There is a wide range of products, including decorative boxes, trays, coasters and bowls. We wanted to buy some pieces as they were so appealing but felt they were too delicate to carry for the journey ahead.

Twice we hired a Shakira with oarsman for forty cents per hour to take us on a ride through the canals, which was most serene and picturesque.

In the town of Srinagar, I couldn't stop myself from entering the numerous rug stores. This time I saw a different type of rug, which absolutely amazed me. Kashmir is world-renowned for their silk carpets. They are made in traditional Persian designs, some silk on cotton, others silk on silk, which were the finest most intricate and pliable rugs, the finest totalling 800 knots per square inch (approx. 5,000 knots per square centimetre). I knew that my father sold silk rugs from Qum in Iran and I wondered why he had never sold Kashmir silk rugs as I felt they were even more beautiful than the Persian.

After eight days, we caught a forty-five-minute flight to Jammu as we didn't want to face the bus trip down the mountain again and from there, we took a train to Delhi.

Indian train travel is an experience in itself, having the largest train network in the world. At every stop, no matter how small, there are people selling every kind of food, drink and everything else imaginable. Sellers walk up and down the platforms and through the trains shouting 'chai, chai', 'coffee, coffee' and offering various sorts of vegetarian and non-vegetarian snacks. The smell of soot from the steam trains permeates through the carriages.

Arriving at New Delhi Central Station, we immediately encountered the largest number of 'Hotel Wallahs'. These were people waiting for arriving trains to try and persuade travellers to follow them to their patron's hotel, where, of course, they were paid a spotter's fee. We were basically mobbed. Fortunately, meeting travellers on the road, we had been recommended a hotel in Paharganj, the area where all of the young travellers stayed. It was within walking distance from the railway station so we escaped the Hotel Wallahs, asked directions and made our own way.

Main Bazaar Road is the hub of Paharganj. It is a long stretch of road opposite the railway station with throngs of people in a lively and chaotic atmosphere. It is only a narrow street, lined with shops, stalls and street sellers selling a wide variety of clothing, accessories, textiles, jewellery, toys, rucksacks, perfumes and souvenirs. Bargaining is the common practice. Lots of small cafés offered a range of both Indian and international cuisines and many affordable hotels and guesthouses catered to backpackers and budget hippie travellers. We were staying in a two-dollar-a-night room, which was relatively clean and we had our own bathroom. It was situated in New Delhi but has more of a feel of being in Old Delhi.

In Paharganj on our second night, as we were walking to the hotel, a young beggar boy approached and asked for rupees. He grabbed onto my legs pleading 'Please, sir.'

I didn't give him anything and then as we got to the hotel, he looked sadly up at me and said 'Tomorrow, sir.'

This was my first encounter with an Indian beggar and these words have always haunted me. He looked so lonely, sad, malnourished and needy. I remember clearly the way he looked at me; those words reminded me of the famous line in *Oliver Twist* when he said, 'Please, sir, can I have some more?' I realised at that moment how privileged and wealthy we were in comparison, having grown up in Australia. Since then, I have always been generous to genuine beggars.

In New Delhi, we discovered Connaught Circle, the financial and business centre as well as the major shopping, dining and entertainment hub. It is a prominent landmark in the centre of New Delhi consisting of two circles: the inner and outer circle, connected by radial roads. The architecture is a blend of Victorian, Colonial and Art Deco. Both circles feature large colonnades, adorned with wide white pillars adding to the grandeur of the circles. We enjoyed walking under these colonnades around both circles, as it was bustling with energy and activities during the day and at night. In the middle of the circle is a large park known as Central Park. It has lots of lush green lawns, trees, flower beds and pathways always filled with Indian families unwinding and enjoying nature's surroundings.

One of the roads leading from the outer circle is called Baba Kharak Singh Marg. Walking along this street is an eye-opener as it has a cluster of government-run emporiums selling traditional handicrafts, artwork and artifacts representing each of the states of India. This was our first introduction to the vast variety of handicrafts being offered throughout India and showed us how different the products of each state were and what to expect as we moved around the country.

On Janpath, another road leading from Connaught is the Tibetan Market, a vibrant shopping strip with lots of small stores selling a diverse and interesting collection of Tibetan and Indian handicrafts, clothing, books, fragrances and jewellery in a bustling and colourful setting.

Our first impressions of Delhi were not very favourable as it was probably a culture shock seeing so many people all congregating together but slowly, it changed the more we observed the Indian lifestyle and what was going on around us in the streets, particularly in the area around our hotel and Connaught Circle. There were so many people in the streets, but we never got the feeling of it being overcrowded and I wrote down at that time that there was relatively little traffic. The population of Delhi in 1975 was 6.2 million whereas today it has 31 million. Now, as the population is more affluent, a larger percentage have cars and with this massive population, the traffic is now choked.

There were two different money-changing scams that went on particularly in the Paharganj area at this time to woo in naïve young tourists. Fortunately, we didn't get caught by these scams as we had been warned about them by travellers on the road. I certainly witnessed this happening but didn't dare intervene for fear of being hurt as these men looked quite ruthless.

The first situation occurred by men standing on corners near a lane, calling out, 'Change money, best rate.' You would be offered about thirty per cent more than from a bank. The tourist would show his money and hold it in his hand. The seller would count off the notes in front of you. Just as you were about to check the counting, the seller would call out 'police coming', grab your money and hand you his, both of you running in different directions. When you stopped to count your money, you would see that every second note was folded in half, so you actually received half of what you were expecting.

The second situation involved travellers' cheques, which were commonly used at that time. Travellers' cheques were issued by banks in various currencies, depending on where you were travelling. They were individually numbered and you would sign one part when collecting from the bank and sign in a second part when cashing in or making a purchase. The signatures needed to match for them to be accepted.

Young tourists would sit in a small café and a young Western couple would join you, or you would join them and you would talk about your travels. In conversation, they would tell you a way in which you could double your money if you had travellers' cheques. They would mention that they were meeting someone soon who they had previously given their travellers' cheques to and that they doubled their money. The naïve tourist would follow this couple who would meet an Indian man further down the street and hand over their travellers' cheques. The naïve tourist would then hand over his and the Indian man would leave, explaining that he would go and collect the money and meet you back in an hour. The Western couple would suddenly disappear and lose themselves in the crowd. Naturally, the dealer never came back and the Western tourists were not seen again. They were part of the scam and would later be paid their commission.

On Main Bazaar Road, we bought a packet of what they call 'mixture', which was a variety of nuts. Ester bit on one and broke a tooth. We panicked as to what to do because all we had seen were dentists sitting on the footpath with a mat in front of them and primitive tools like plyers. I called the Australian embassy, and they referred us to a dentist in the diplomatic quarter.

The diplomatic quarter was a beautiful suburb in New Delhi where the embassies are situated and most are designed in the style of the countries they represented. There are also beautiful large private homes with manicured gardens. The surgery was in the dentist's modern home, which was tastefully furnished. To our surprise, the dental surgery had the latest equipment with classical music playing in the background. The dentist had studied in England and was obviously upper class. He did a perfect job repairing Ester's tooth. As we left, he was talking to another Indian gentleman, and I remember his words: 'We must get together for a musical evening soon.' A remnant of the British Raj.

The caste system has been deeply ingrained in India's social hierarchy for thousands of years and that is why there is a vast difference in the wealth and lifestyles of the large population.

The caste system works with the Brahmins who traditionally hold the role of priests and scholars as the highest caste. Below them are the Kshatriyas, who are the warriors and ruling class; third in line are the Vaishyas, who are involved in business and commerce. Below them are the Shudras, who perform manual labour and service. Further down the chain are the Dalits or 'untouchables', who have historically been considered so low in social status that they have been excluded from mainstream society and have been subjected to discrimination.

The Indian government has been trying to eradicate this caste system to promote social, wealth and employment equality but it is still a big challenge and is a concern in India's ongoing social and political discourse. It is so undemocratic and discriminating. However, I have seen a huge change in the caste system during the fifty years that I have been travelling to India, especially with the 'untouchables', who are now more and more accepted as part of society.

Even though we were staying cheaply in Paharganj, we had been on the road for quite a while and money was running low. As we still wanted to travel on, I did a scam that I am certainly not proud of, but we were young and foolish. I can't quite remember where we put our baggage, but we caught a taxi, checked into a different hotel in Paharganj without bags and told reception that the taxi drove off with them. We stayed the night and the next morning, we went to the police and told them a massive lie about the taxi taking our bags. They asked what the taxi looked like. I said it was a black taxi with a yellow roof (they all were). They then asked if he could describe the driver. I said he was a Sikh with a turban (basically all the taxi drivers were Sikh). They gave us a police statement which I sent off to my travel insurance company and made a claim. This gave us enough money to keep on the road.

From Delhi, we travelled by train to Jaipur, the Pink City, where we stayed in a government tourist bungalow for three days. These bungalows were set up in British Colonial times when the British established a network of rest houses and bungalows across India to cater for the needs of travellers, government officials and British officers stationed in different regions. There was no network of hotels for foreign tourists during these times and travel through India was arduous. I wondered if my grandfather had stayed in these in 1936. When India gained independence in 1947, the Indian Government took over the management of them and developed them further to promote a budget-friendly and comfortable place to stay to promote tourism. They are simple accommodations, clean, neat and inexpensive, still frequented by young backpackers.

Jaipur is a beautiful city that I now visit regularly. It would be my favourite city in India. All the buildings in the old walled city are painted pink and have a distinct Rajasthan design. The women wear the most beautiful colourful saris; the men wear beautiful turbans and traditional clothing. There are monkeys jumping across the tops of buildings and some of the people ride very colourfully decorated elephants. The buildings outside the walled city are quite stunning and the Rambagh Palace is a standout former palace of the Maharajah, now one of the top hotels in India.

Amazingly, we bumped into David and Kathy, our friends from Mykonos, in Jaipur and had a wonderful few days exploring the sights of Jaipur together, mainly following each other in bicycle rickshaws.

We were contemplating where to travel next. Do we go south to Bombay and down to the most renowned hippie hangout of Goa? Or do we visit Agra to see the Taj Mahal? The Taj Mahal was east and on the way to the ancient city of Varanasi, which the travel guide *Overland to India and Australia* described as 'one of the oldest continuous cities in the world'. It was a significant spiritual centre not to be missed so we decided to head there as it was in the direction of Australia.

From Jaipur, we took a four-hour train ride to visit Agra and the Taj Mahal. It was the most magnificent construction we had ever seen and not at all overrated. This translucent white marble mausoleum with its intricate carvings and inlaid gemstones radiated beauty and perfection. Being surrounded by symmetrical manicured gardens makes it appear to be floating on water. It was built in the seventeenth century by Emperor Shah Jahan in memory of his wife Mumtaz Mahal as a promise he had made to her. It took twenty-two years to construct by 20,000 workers. Shah Jahan never wanted this beauty repeated so he chopped off the thumbs of the two architects that designed it. It is worthily considered as one of the New Seven Wonders of the World. We visited the Taj Mahal about three times. It was so magnificent that one visit was not enough.

The other sights of Agra that we really enjoyed were the Agra Fort, which is a massive red sandstone fort housing palaces, mosques and courtyards, and the fascinating Fatehpur Sikri, a desert city fifteen kilometres out of the city, a showcase of Mughal art and architecture.

Our next adventure was to visit Varanasi so we took a long arduous uncomfortable train ride there. Varanasi is one of the oldest and most fascinating cities in the world and has been continuously inhabited for over 3,000 years. It is the spiritual heart of India, the holiest city for Hindus. We found a room in the old city, which is steeped in history. The old city hits you with a sensory overload of sights, sounds and smells and is a labyrinth of narrow alleys, ancient temples, a bustling market selling food, spices, religious items, household items, handicrafts and the famous Benares silk, which is handwoven with elaborate patterns and known throughout India for its quality and beauty popularly used for Sarees on special occasions. The ghats (which are the steps leading down to the Ganges River) are on the edge of the old city. There are small basic budget hotels spread throughout and small inexpensive restaurants catering to the young travellers that were venturing there.

Taking a small rowboat with an oarsman along the Ganges at sunrise is one of the most amazing experiences one cannot imagine or envisage.

The sun can be seen rising from the horizon on the opposite side of the river and as you slowly travel along the river, you view visitors from all over India and local pilgrims bathing, drinking the holy Ganges water, washing their clothes and giving offerings to the gods whilst seeing funeral pyres billow smoke into the air as bodies burn.

Little did I know at that time that Delhi, Agra, Jaipur and Varanasi would become my future. It is these four cities that I have visited more than 100 times and have formed the backbone of Hali, my rug business, providing me and my family the lifestyle I had hoped for.

From Varanasi, we trained to the town of Khajuraho, famous for its complex group of temples built between the ninth and eleventh centuries made of sandstone in what was called the Nagara style. It is a UNESCO World Heritage Site set over a large area originally consisting of eighty-five temples of which only about twenty-five remain. These temples are adorned with thousands of elaborate carvings and intricate detailing. One of the most striking features of the Khajuraho temples is the explicit depiction of sexual themes. These erotic sculptures are believed to represent the celebration of the human body and fertility and obviously gain a lot of tourists' attention.

We headed back to Varanasi so we could further our adventure and bus over the border to Nepal.

Chapter 14

The bus ride from Varanasi to Kathmandu in Nepal took a gruelling sixteen hours. In Kathmandu, young hippie travellers from all over the world stayed in a street appropriately called Freak Street as it had inexpensive guesthouses, cafes and shops so that's where we stayed and hung out. However, my first impression of Kathmandu was of disappointment. It was a very dirty city, much dirtier than Indian cities. On the side of the road were not only animal faeces but also human faeces and the locals regularly spit or blow phlegm on the pavements.

All the restaurants played Western pop music. We were continually approached with, 'Want to buy postcards? Very cheap,' 'Want to buy hashish?' 'Want Tibetan carpets? Come to my shop.' We did not experience this in India as it was so chill. We encountered more tourists in Kathmandu than in any other part of Asia so far.

It took us a few days to accept these annoying approaches and then we started to enjoy the history, food and people of Nepal. In Kathmandu, we hired bicycles and rode to the nearby towns of Patan and Bhaktapur, which were quite beautiful, ancient and dotted with elaborate pagoda-style temples. Riding through the wheat fields, the farmers were gathering up the wheat and we were gobsmacked by the backdrop of more beautiful temples and the stunning snow-capped Himalayan Mountains in the distance. The houses in Nepal have a distinct design. They are solid houses constructed from brick and stone with wooden eaves, shutters, balconies and doors all beautifully carved with great detail.

There were many rug stores in Kathmandu selling mainly Tibetan rugs. My parents always had traditional Persian rugs in their home and as I have pointed out throughout my overland travels, I kept being drawn to looking at rugs. I had never seen Tibetan rugs before and we were both attracted to them. We decided to buy our first rug and purchased a navy-blue Tibetan rug that was 160 centimetres by ninety centimetres with a colourful dragon running the length of it. We arranged for it to be shipped home. We weren't confident that they would ever ship it, took the risk and yes, it did arrive.

A Thangka is a Tibetan Buddhist hanging scroll made of fabric that is hand-painted in fine detail by Tibetan artists, usually using mineral pigments and gold detailing, depicting various subjects relating to Tibetan Buddhism. The Tibetans believe them to have spiritual significance, using them as a visual aid in meditation. There were many for sale and as we realised that we were now heading home, we purchased a beautiful one. It was light, rolled up and easy to carry. It wasn't a rug but certainly held a similar handmade tribal vibe that attracted me.

Chapter 15

It was a long journey from Kathmandu to Calcutta on the east coast of India, but we bused over the border back into India and trained our way to Calcutta.

Howrah Railway Station, Calcutta was the busiest railway station I have ever entered. There were swarms of people heading in all directions. The first thing that struck me once leaving the station was the rickshaws. Unlike rickshaws we had seen so far, which were all bicycle rickshaws, these were drawn by men running as they pulled you along. The traffic was more congested; people were literally everywhere and the buildings were more dilapidated than the rest of India. It looked so much poorer and seemed like a city in chaos, probably what I had imagined India to be like before having been there.

We didn't stay long in Calcutta but wanted to explore the laid-back town of Puri, which was down the east coast, another spot that had found its way as a hippie destination, so we made our way back to the crowded Howrah Station and caught a train south.

Puri was not very developed nor overcrowded but a beautiful village where the locals were involved mainly in fishing and handicrafts. It's renowned for the Jagannath Temple, a pilgrimage sight for Hindus that brought them tourism. Intricate carvings depicting scenes of Hindu mythology adorn the temple. Small figurines of the stone and wood carvings sculptures, which were found on the Jagannath Temple, are sold to tourists. Puri also has beautiful colourful applique wall hangings, of which we purchased one and large colourful applique beach umbrellas.

It is set in the Bay of Bengal with serene clean beaches. We found a small guest house near the beach, ate lots of fresh fish in the local cafes and spent lots of time relaxing on the beach under one of the beautiful colourful umbrellas that were dotted along the beach.

After a relaxing ten days, we headed to Madras, a sleepy white city in Southern India that we didn't find very exciting and caught a train back to Calcutta to continue our journey East to Burma.

It was time to leave India. No other country had interested or excited me more. I loved the vibe of the country from the first moment the soldier at the border welcomed us to 'Mother India'. It was a magical country so full of contrasts. Every day was like an adventure. Something was bound to happen, whether it be visual or funny. It is often called the 'subcontinent of diversity' and this is what captivated me from the first moment. It has a fascinating blend of ancient traditions and modernity. Beautiful palaces and architectural marvels like the Taj Mahal contrast the poorest of shanty towns. It's full of breathtaking landscapes and friendly warm people, and I loved the food. Each state of India is like a country of its own. The architecture varies, landscape changes, traditional clothing varies, food is unique to each state and languages are different. Hindi was introduced as the national language but in fact, English is the most widely spoken language.

India is unique and has a special charm that one cannot experience anywhere else and it has such a lovely peaceful feeling even though nothing works efficiently or fast.

The book *Overland to India and Australia* described India at the time as follows: 'India is confusion, chaos, filth, beauty, infinite variety, poverty, fabulous riches, spiritual enlightenment, corruption, insanity, cows and 500 million people. It contains some of the most beautiful and sordid scenes on earth. Everything happens on the street, very little is hidden... Never expect anything to work on time or efficiently, indeed when you get to India, Slowdown.'

You couldn't help but slow down – that was the pace of life in India.

Changing money at a bank took about an hour. To buy bus or train tickets took longer; to ask directions was useless. I wrote to my parents at the time that my first impressions were that India was not as poor as I imagined. There were not that many beggars and everyone looked well-fed. It was, however, dirty but if you were willing to pay a bit more, you could find good clean restaurants and hotels that are for middle-class Indians. We were living in very clean conditions and eating beautiful food for about US$65 per week.

We had travelled around India for close to four months and I remember nearly every day of this first magical trip.

Chapter 16

Our next stop was Burma but as it wasn't possible to travel overland, we caught a flight from Calcutta to Rangoon.

Burma was a socialist country under very strict authoritarian military rule. There was nationalisation of all major industries and no trade with the outside world. Tourists were only permitted a seven-day visa. Virtually every tourist was young and carried a duty-free bottle of Johnny Walker Red and a carton of Dunhill as they entered Rangoon, the capital city. We did the same. Tourists sold them at the black market on arrival for a 600% profit and this gave them enough money to last the entire week. You needed to change money legally, so we changed five dollars each and with the cost of the whiskey and cigarettes, the week cost us twenty-five dollars in total.

Rangoon was quite dilapidated. It looked as though no construction work had been undertaken for many years; however, it retained much of its historic charm with a mix of British Colonial architecture and traditional pagodas lining the streets. We found the Burmese to be extremely friendly and spoke English very well. We were greeted and waved at wherever we went.

The stores were virtually empty and it seemed like the entire country survived via the black market. At night, there were extensive street markets where all types of smuggled and second-hand goods would be sold, which the government obviously tolerated. Items such as old watches, cigarette lighters, transistor radios, car stereos, Nescafé, Ovaltine, toothpaste and pharmaceuticals. In fact, everything imaginable.

We stayed in Rangoon for three days and then caught a gruelling seventeen-hour steam train to Mandalay, a smaller city abounding with beautiful pagodas and monasteries. We then travelled by boat up the Irrawaddy River to a small town that was renowned for having the largest bell in the world, known as the Great Bell of Dhammazedi. Not many travellers ventured this far and I distinctly remember that when we stopped to look at something, people would surround us, stare, point and laugh.

Making sure we got back to Rangoon within the seven days, we then flew to Bangkok where we only stayed a couple of days. It was more expensive than the countries we had been travelling through and was the first place since Europe where everything seemed to work efficiently – and we couldn't believe that they had air conditioning in the hotel rooms! We would have loved to stay longer but our money was running low and as mentioned, it was more expensive, so we decided to head down to Penang for some beach relaxation. We trained to Malaysia and the island of Penang. What a difference the trains in Southeast Asia were to those in Asia. We were suddenly in a modern fast comfortable airconditioned train that took us to Kuala Lumpur, switched to Butterworth and then a ferry across to the island.

We slept in a small hotel in Georgetown that had a lane outside of our window. It was hot without air conditioning, so we left the window slightly open. I woke up in the middle of the night as I heard a noise. I looked up and saw a hand reaching in and pulling the strap of my camera. The camera disappeared out of the window. I jumped up, ran out and chased him down the lane. He dropped my camera; I retrieved it and all good. We slept with the window closed in a hot room for the remainder of our stay!

Penang was a gorgeous island and it was nice to kick back and relax on the beach after the continual and busy travel that we had been doing. The historic city of Georgetown is a stunning blend of well-preserved Colonial architecture. These were recognised as a UNESCO World

Heritage Site later in 2008. There was a diverse mixture of ethnic groups like Malays, Chinese and Indians. We thoroughly enjoyed the lively street markets and the delicious Malay cuisine which was very different to the foods we had enjoyed through India, Nepal and Burma.

After about a week of relaxing on the beach of Penang, we trained again in luxury to Singapore for a few days. Here, we were confronted by loads of high-rise buildings, hotels, strip shopping and ultra-modern shopping centres. It was like we were in a giant supermarket. We moved on quickly as this was not our vibe and we wanted to explore Indonesia, completing our two-year journey in Bali that we heard from various travellers was extremely cheap, the people were friendly and the beaches were beautiful. We flew to Jakarta and immediately bused our way through the island of Java as Jakarta was a hectic overcrowded city that didn't have any appeal to us.

Halfway through the island of Java is the city of Jogjakarta. We stayed there and thoroughly enjoyed our three-day stay. It was a unique and captivating town that was different and had a rich cultural and historical significance. We explored the town on the back of a rickshaw, visiting the sultan's palace, the grandeur of the Javanese court and a factory that produced batik textiles. Batik is a fabric with intricate traditional Indonesian designs drawn onto it. Hot wax is applied to the areas of the fabric that intend to remain undyed and after dyeing, the fabric is boiled to remove the wax, revealing the final design.

The island of Sumba is an Indonesian island that produces handwoven blankets using an old-age technique passed on through the generations on a horizontal loom. They are not soft like a normal blanket but more like a textile or rug. Sumba blankets are hand-dyed with symbolic representations of mythical creatures, animals and ancestral motifs. Many have tribal Ikat patterns, often in bold, eye-catching colours of red and indigo, reminding us of the colourful Berber rugs we had seen in Morocco. As they were quite unique and as we had never seen them before, we couldn't resist purchasing one from a handicraft store in

Jogjakarta. Was it because my admiration of tribal rugs and my interest in rugs generally was growing?

We bused through the rest of Java and took a ferry across to Bali, our last stop before finally flying home. Kuta Beach was relatively undiscovered on the tourist map. It was only a small village with a very relaxed untouched atmosphere. There was only basic accommodation and only a few local 'warungs' where you could eat. If you walked towards Legian, it was through rice paddies with cows, chickens and pigs roaming freely. It was at this time that travellers like us were beginning to discover Bali and by the late seventies, it became a bustling tourist stop.

We met up with a few friends from Australia there and one night, we all took magic mushrooms. We ran in the dark into the surf at Kuta and played in the waves like it was a giant bubble bath. In hindsight this was a terrible idea as Bali is infamous for having dangerous currents, with people drowning there almost daily. Fortunately, we all survived without issue.

Melbourne was next. Our final stop. Home.

We were excited to see our families and friends but at the same time, we realised that our fantasy, indefinite carefree life of the past two years had come to an end. We were heading home not really realising what was in store for us next.

PART TWO

Chapter 17

We returned to Australia in late April 1976, just short of two years on the road. Arriving home was overwhelming and a shock for both of us; our adventure and freedom of the past two years was now over. I was penniless and in debt to my father, so we stayed with friends and slowly found ourselves moving back into our Melbourne social group. The hardest part was the realisation that we needed to start working, find a home, retrieve our furniture that had been in storage for two years and purchase cars as Melbourne was a difficult city to live in without a vehicle.

Fortunately, I had an acquaintance, Marc Cywinski, from my days in the rag trade who had been very successful with a company called Cherry Lane and offered me a job working in his stock room. This was my only ever full-time job working as an employee and became my last. Ester had been a legal secretary before we went away and started working for a solicitor in North Melbourne. We slowly got back onto our feet and rented a house in Elsternwick.

My brother Nick had returned to Australia about eight months earlier and opened a women's fashion store in the Moonee Ponds Market. This was a new market concept as each stall was a permanent fixture that you fitted out and your stock remained as it had a locking roller door. After several months of working at Cherry Lane, an opportunity arose to open a similar stall at the new Preston Market. Once again, Nick and I went into partnership, opening a Preston Market outlet. I looked after Preston and Nick remained in Moonee Ponds. Due to our previous contacts in the industry, we were able to obtain good stock, especially Cherry Lane, which was extremely popular and we had it exclusively for the markets. We called our business 'Babes' and over time, we opened free-standing stores, eventually having five quite successful fashion outlets.

In January 1977, my daughter Rebecca was born. We called her Becky from the start and this has stuck. Once you have a child, life changes and, might I say, for the better. It was love at first sight and I couldn't wait to get home from work to see my special little person. I now had a serious responsibility.

Chapter 18

The travel bug was still with me. I was drawn to visiting different countries that all had unique characteristics and ways of life. Each country has its own culture, customs, features, clothing, traditions, language, food, music, dance, festivals, architecture, geography, living standards, ways of occupying the day, politics and more. It fascinated me and I made the decision to see as much of this amazing vast world as I could. The thought of not travelling again or not for ages was not on my radar.

Ester and I pondered over where to go and whether we could with a small baby as it was December 1977 and Rebecca was eleven months old and not yet walking. The desire was too strong and we felt capable and able to travel with a small child. India was the place that had taken our heart and we wanted to explore more of it as from our previous visit, we realised that India was like a multitude of countries rolled into one.

We decided to go to Goa as during the 1970s it was the hippie centre of the world and we hadn't yet explored it. So off we ventured, baby in tow.

Anjuna Beach in Goa was like another world as there seemed to be no laws. Each person was able to act, to dress or to undress as they pleased. It had beautiful beaches and there was a relaxed attitude towards drugs. Full moon beach parties were the biggest event and other beach parties every few nights were real happenings that went all night. Bands played on the beach, chai stalls, freak food, drugs. You would take along a mat and a blanket and set yourself up for the night. There was an incredible

Sunday flea market; nudity and the waft of hashish chillums were everywhere.

We found a cute room with a small kitchen area so that we could cook clean good food for Becky. It also had a small bath to bathe her in. The toilet didn't have a flush, but your poo went into an angled hole that led outside to a narrow drain. The local pigs would be waiting, licking their lips as they would lap up your faeces. Since that time, I have never eaten bacon in India!

We participated in all the parties that were happening and in the soft drugs that were surrounding us. We knew a few friends from Australia there, some also with small children. It was a blast and we partied and relaxed on the beach for six weeks. Rebecca took her first steps there!

Goa is quite different to the rest of India as it was colonised by the Portuguese. This began in the sixteenth century and lasted for approximately 400 years. It was a vital centre of trade and commerce for the Portuguese as they established a monopoly over the spice trade and controlled it through the Goan ports. After Indian independence from the British in 1947, Goa remained under Portuguese rule and it wasn't until 1961 that the Indian army invaded Goa and ended this rule. During their reign, they constructed forts, churches and houses in typical Portuguese style, many of which are still standing, so Goa instantly has a different feel to the rest of India. The Portuguese missionaries were very active in converting many of the local population to Christianity; therefore, Goa has a significant Christian population.

On the 16th of January 1978, the Indian government passed the High Denomination Bank Note Act whereby all currency notes of value 1,000 rupees or more were made worthless. This was whilst we were in Goa and the public had until the 19th of January to sign a three-page document showing proof as to how they had obtained the notes legally after which they would become worthless. We had a couple of 1,000-rupee notes that we had exchanged at a bank and still had the receipt, so we ventured into the bank in town to cash them in. Talk about queues and chaos.

Crowds and crowds of people stood in lines. A day was wasted as we stood in line, filled in the three-page document and claimed our money.

Black money is money that has been received from earnings without any tax being paid on it. Those who had large denomination notes that were black money couldn't simply go to a bank to deposit them or exchange them as it would lead to questions from the taxation department, so they lost the full value of the black money they had stored. The State Bank of India later announced that twenty-five per cent of the total currency notes did not return to the banking system.

This act was repeated in November 2016 when Prime Minister Modi announced that 500 and 1,000 rupees would be scrapped in a bid to flush out the tax evaders once again as only five per cent of Indians fill in tax returns and pay tax. These notes accounted for eighty-six per cent of cash in circulation so it severely hurt those hoarding black money. There were cash shortages for weeks as the highest legal denomination was the 100 rupee note, which equates to about two Australian dollars until the new 500 and 1,000 rupee notes were produced and placed into circulation. Coincidently, my son Dan and his wife Emma were in India during this time.

The World Bank estimated at the time that the black-market economy of India amounted to 23.2 per cent of India's total economy. GST is the most successful tax in India as it cannot be avoided. It's applied to everything purchased and amounts to twenty-eight per cent of the tax collected by the Indian government.

On this trip, we flew in and out of Bombay, which we hadn't visited previously (now called Mumbai, its original Indian name), another amazing city. We stayed in the area known as Colaba, which was a vibrant neighbourhood of Bombay with markets, street vendors and great Indian food. It had retained a feeling of the British Raj with its charming buildings from the British era and was where the Gateway of India and the famous Taj Mahal Palace Hotel were along a beautiful seafront. Close to the Gateway was a small park where entertainers of all kinds gathered. We saw snake charmers, trainers with monkeys, others with bears on a chain, magicians and acrobats. The acrobats were usually a family with their children performing quite amazing aerial feats.

The Colaba Causeway was a main street that had lots of fashion, shoe stores and restaurants and was always bustling with throngs of people. There was a restaurant called Leopold which was an inexpensive restaurant with quirky memorabilia adorning the walls and a retro charm with vintage décor and wooden furniture. This restaurant had a mixture of both Indian and Western food and was the place where all the young travellers would meet, eat, discuss their travels, score some hashish or simply hang out. It gained international attention in the novel *Shantaram* in the early 1980s as it was the place he would regularly go to and mention in his novel.

Unfortunately, Leopold was attacked in 2008 by heavily armed Pakistani militants who opened fire on the patrons and staff, resulting in a horrific scene. The most well-documented attack was at the Taj Mahal Palace Hotel, only one street away. Leopold is still the place where young travellers congregate.

The other hippie hangout was a juice bar around the corner known as Diptis. It had a great range of fresh juices. It was only a small store with not much seating but it was always busy with young travellers mingling outside.

Behind the Taj Hotel was a small shopping street that sold lots of handicrafts, with several shops selling Kashmir silk carpets. I couldn't resist entering these stores and admiring the carpets. Now that I was back at home and had seen my father's rug store, which I found to be quite uninteresting, I took some photos of the beautiful Kashmir silk rugs that had taken my attention. Arriving home, I showed him the photos, but he was quite set in his ways. He only wanted Persian rugs, showing no interest. This frustrated me as I felt so sure that they would sell well in Australia; however, the thought of importing rugs myself and selling them in Australia was still not at all on my radar, even though I kept being drawn to rugs wherever I had seen them on my earlier travels through the East.

Living this alternative lifestyle in Goa did not change my desire to be successful in business. In one of the handicraft stores on the same street as the Kashmir rug stores, I found beautiful ivory products and could see a business opportunity. The range consisted of jewellery boxes, ashtrays, cigarette boxes, small vases and walking canes made of wood with small pieces of ivory stuck to them covering the wood. I purchased a collection and placed them in my father's store for sale. I was surprised that he allowed me to sell them in his store. They sold successfully and helped cover a large cost of the trip. They were beautiful but I didn't keep any for myself, thinking I would buy more next trip but not long after, the Indian government placed a ban on the export of all ivory.

I really enjoyed our time in Goa but after returning to Australia, I realised that the hippie lifestyle was coming to an end for me. I wanted to move on, get involved in business and be successful at it. I had the responsibility of having a daughter and wanted to able to give her the best education and a comfortable lifestyle in our own home. Our alternative and free-spirited lifestyle was not going to provide it. Ester was still keen on living this way. It was clear our lives were heading in different directions, so we went through a painful split. Our marriage unfortunately ended in April 1978 when Becky was fifteen months old.

It hurt me deeply parting ways, but I was still young and knew I had a future ahead of me; I needed to pick up my life and move on.

Chapter 19

I would visit my father's shop regularly and as mentioned found it to be quite uninteresting. It lacked style and variety. It wasn't doing well; I wanted to help him in any way I could, and I knew that I could.

In the middle of 1978, I told my father and uncle that I had seen beautiful rugs during my time in Afghanistan that were very different to what they were selling and I was sure they would sell successfully in Australia where I had never seen any. I told them if they financed a trip for me, I would buy a selection of beautiful rugs for them. My uncle suggested that I travel with my cousin Theo (also his nephew) who would buy for him and I would choose a selection for my father.

So off we went to Kabul, Afghanistan on my first-ever rug-buying trip. In Kabul, we found a couple of good carpet wholesalers with a huge selection and purchased rugs from them. It was fun and exciting. I loved carefully selecting the rugs, making sure that they lay flat and that the borders were straight. We chose the designs and colours we thought were the most interesting and would sell best.

The buying experience and being in an exotic city were certainly a very different experience to the fashion samples I had purchased earlier in Europe.

Afghan rugs are quite different to the traditional Persian rugs that my father and uncle sold. They are hand-knotted on a traditional vertical loom with local Afghan mountain wool, which is quite thick and solid, creating a relatively high pile. The colours are rich and vibrant, which is achieved using natural dyes derived from plants and fruit mostly in deep reds, blues and earth tones. The designs are mainly geometrical with intricate designs of hexagons, diamonds, stars and stylised floral motifs.

I never envisaged at that time that my life would eventually be engulfed in the rug industry as from what I had seen from my father and uncle's experience, rugs only appealed to a small minority of the public as most Australians had wall-to-wall carpeting throughout their homes. This was the trend and I didn't realise that it would soon change.

Being so close to India, I couldn't resist stopping off before going home so together we flew to Bombay and on to Mysore in southern India to visit a hill station called Ootacamund, 125 kilometres away up a mountain, as we heard it was a spectacular place to visit and chill out for a couple of days. Hill stations were set up by the British at high altitudes as a relief to the heat. Ooty was established by the British in the 1820s.

We met a friendly American girl on the flight who was doing the same, so we told her to join us as we were going to hire a car with a driver to take us there. In the small dusty airport, there was only one car hire place and the manager told us that he had no cars left 'but don't worry, sir, as I will call for my own personal car and driver to take you.'

We waited a half hour or so and a 1960 two-door Triumph Herald arrived, a very small car. The three of us climbed in and off we went. It started to rain heavily, and we told him to put on the wipers. Perfect, there was only one working windscreen wiper, and it was on the passenger side! Luckily it stopped raining as we began ascending the steep mountain. The car began to drive slower and slower until it finally came to a stop. It could not climb the steep mountain. The three of us had to get out so the car could go forward. It didn't help much as it could still only crawl up without us. We took our bags out of the car and told him to leave. We had had enough. We waited by the side of the road and fortunately, a car stopped and gave us a lift to the top where we checked into the Savoy Hotel, a British Style hotel, a remnant of the British occupation.

The mountains surrounding Ooty are known as the Nilgiri Hills with peaks ranging between 1700 to 2600 metres. For centuries, the Toda tribe lived in isolation in the Nilgiri Hills surrounding Ooty and were a small simple rural community, grazing their water buffalos and growing a variety of different crops. The British moved them out of Ooty and established the Nilgiri Biosphere Reserve, a UNESCO World Heritage Site nearby where they still live in traditional Toda huts, which are a distinct barrel-shaped form made of wood, rattan, bamboo and grass. They still tend to their buffalos but the crops that they now grow are 'English vegetables' like carrots, potatoes and cabbage. We went to visit the reserve and were drawn to the beautiful embroidery work that the women created on the shawls that were worn by both genders, called *puthkuli*. We also thought the silver jewellery that they made to wear during religious rituals consisting of silver belts necklaces, bracelets, earrings and anklets were very interesting and distinctive. The pieces were quite heavy with the use of silver beads often threaded onto a silver wire-plaited cord or intricately laced together with stunning silver buckles. We couldn't resist purchasing them as they were unique and aesthetic, so we bought forty kilos of the jewellery and took them back to Australia, which we then sold.

In those days, airline security was very slack so we carried the jewellery onto the plane, lifting the heavy two bags up into the overhead compartments. As with the ivory, I placed the pieces I had bought in my father's shop and they all sold quickly.

This time, my father loved the rugs. He thought the designs and colours were so different to what he was familiar with but could see that they would appeal to a certain demographic of his clientele. Both he and my uncle had great success selling them.

Rugs were obviously in my blood!

Chapter 20

Not long after the Afghan rug purchase, my father needed to go to the hospital for a few days for tests as he had continual pain in his left leg, and the doctors wanted to ascertain the cause. The shop was a one-man show but it did offer my father a modest income so I told my brother that I would look after it for a few days while he ran our clothing stores. They gave my father a myelogram, which is a procedure whereby they inject dye into the spinal cord to evaluate the spinal cord, nerve roots and structure. These have now been replaced by non-invasive MRI machines. Unfortunately, he had complications as there was a large blood clot in his spine, the dye bursting it and spreading the blood throughout his vertebrae. Later, he had microsurgery to remove the blood that had spread through his spine but it was unsuccessful and sadly, he ended up in a wheelchair.

I looked after the shop for a few months and when we realised our father could no longer work, we decided to close it down. Fortunately, the lease had only three months left so I placed signs on the window 'closing down sale' and business started to boom. I then put small ads in the newspapers; it became busier and busier and I five-folded this little business. This was before there were any rug closing-down sales in Melbourne, which later became a very common thing through the eighties. Stocks began to run low, so I managed to get more rugs on consignment from a wholesaler in Sydney, a small wholesaler in Melbourne called Mr Aloumi and my uncle. It became so busy I employed my friend Carl to help me and when I finally closed the door, I was able to fit all the remaining stock in the boot of my car, which was a small BMW 3 series.

During this sale time, a well-dressed gentleman entered the store and asked how my father was as he had heard that he wasn't well. He told me he had purchased several carpets from him, had become somewhat of a friend and mentioned he would like another silk rug and please send his regards to my father. He selected a silk carpet for $3,000 and handed me a loose cheque, which he signed. I gave him the rug without even asking for his identification as he was such a smooth talker. He walked out with the rug and of course, it was a false cheque – rug gone, no money, lesson learnt. I have never allowed this to happen again. I was still naïve and young.

As my understanding of the rug trade grew, so did my opportunities. For several Saturdays, a man would frequent the shop, often spending considerable time inspecting the rugs. After a few weeks, he introduced himself. His name was Greg Mallyon and he worked for the Council of Adult Education. He asked if I would like to teach a course on oriental rugs and carpets. A laugh escaped my lips. 'Me? I don't know enough.'

He looked at me seriously. He meant business and said, 'You know more than anyone that's walked into this shop and I'll give you six months to prepare.'

I saw this as a great challenge so I took it on, reading all the rug books I could, gathering information and preparing notes.

Before continuing, I should distinguish between the terminology 'rug' and 'carpet' as they are often used interchangeably. The word 'rug' in the industry refers to a loose-fitting floor covering that is smaller than six square metres. A 'carpet' refers to one that is larger than six square metres but still loose-fitting. I tend to use the word rug more often as the general public tends to think that the word carpet refers to wall-to-wall carpeting.

On my next trip to India, my first trip when I entered the world of rugs (which I will discuss in the next chapter), I took slides of the rug-making steps from dyeing, spinning, knotting, clipping and washing of rugs and started the first ever course on oriental rugs in Australia. I continued teaching it for the next ten years.

It began in 1980 and was a six-week introductory course held in the evening at the Council of Education on Flinders Street. Nervously with very sweaty palms and blushing for my first few lectures, I would discuss the main areas of rug making being Iran, Afghanistan, Caucasia (Russian), Turkey, India and Pakistan. I would explain how they were made, what fibres were used and the various classifications of rugs – city, village or tribal rugs – supporting this by showing the slides on a large screen. I would bring along rugs of the various types I described.

The industry has changed greatly since those days as Caucasian rugs are no longer being produced, Afghan rug production is totally disrupted by the Taliban and the industry in Turkey has virtually disappeared. Looking back at my slides now, I can see many small children weaving on the looms. Child labour! But it was never brought to our attention in those days.

For my second year of teaching, I moved the course to the Persian Carpet Warehouse, which is the first rug store I became involved in and is discussed in the chapter following. It was difficult taking samples to Flinders Street and by conducting the course in my store, I had every style of rug at my fingertips to show my students. The students were a variety of younger and middle-aged women and a few married couples.

Later, Greg and I became friends and even spent time in India together.

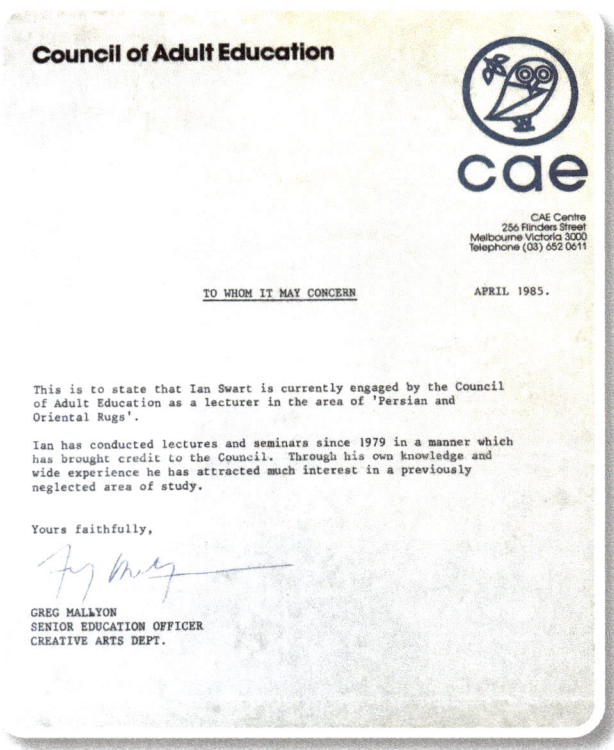

Chapter 21

I realised rugs had a future. My timing was perfect as this was the time when people were moving away from fitting out their homes with wall-to-wall carpets to polishing their floorboards, specifically in Victorian and Edwardian homes that had beautiful Baltic pine floorboards. I decided to enter the rug business so at the end of 1978, Nick and I sold our clothing stores and went our separate ways.

Nick went to work for his father-in-law and established the Fun Factory, an entertainment centre at the Capitol Bakeries Building in South Yarra, which his father-in-law owned, and I opened my first rug store in April 1979 called Eastern Rug Distributors and soon after changed to The Persian Carpet Warehouse in South Melbourne in partnership with my uncle Coenie who still owned his rug shop at the Southern Cross.

Our store was in a beautiful old church building on Dorcas Street, South Melbourne. It was quite unique with detailed stained-glass windows along the sides and a perfect space in between to hang rugs for display with a massive high-timbered sloped ceiling. As the floor space was large we would require lots of large stacks of rugs in various sizes.

To purchase the large amount of stock needed, my uncle and I flew to Europe to purchase carpets from an old friend of his who was a wholesaler of rugs in Amsterdam, and from the world's largest carpet wholesaler at the time, a company in London called Kelaty.

We bought a mixture of Persian, Turkish, Caucasian, Afghan, Pakistani and Indian rugs and at the time of opening, it was Australia's largest handmade carpet store with the widest selection.

We had an amazing Middle Eastern opening function serving Middle Eastern food. It was extremely well attended and we received a wonderful and positive reaction.

Even though my father and uncle dealt in Persian rugs, this was the first time my uncle had purchased Indian rugs. He was amazed at the Indian carpets and thought they were so perfect. He sometimes couldn't distinguish between the actual Persians and these Indian copies. I thought if we went direct, surely we could buy better than purchasing through Europe. No one in Australia was importing Persian-style rugs from India. At that time, all I knew was that the rugs were made in and around the city of Varanasi.

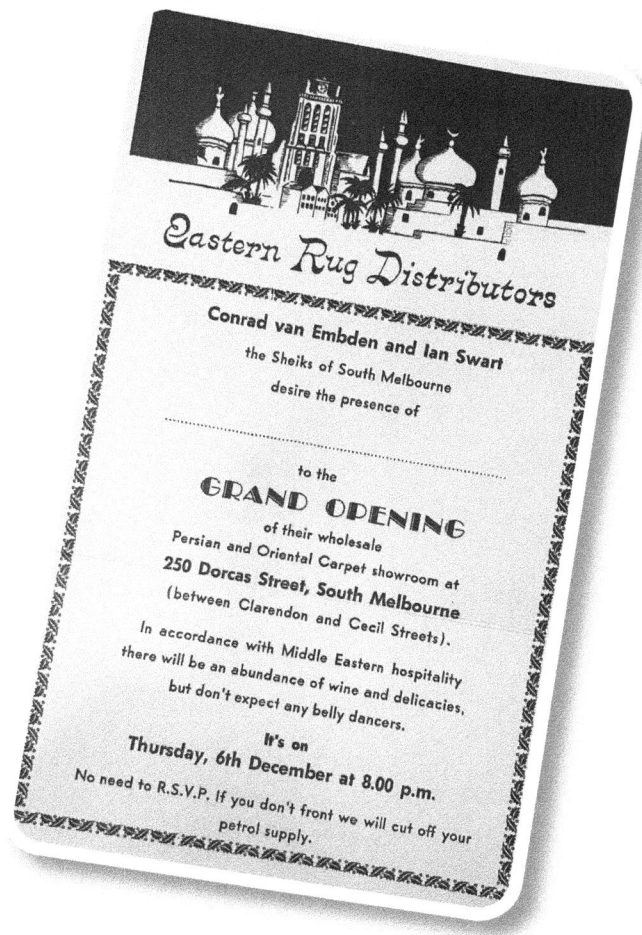

Chapter 22

I flew to Delhi and on to Varanasi in late 1979 and through luck, this trip changed my life!

I was sitting in the coffee shop at the Varanasi Hotel and had booked a taxi to take me to the rug-making villages, which were about sixty kilometres away but had no idea who to see. I was reading a Persian carpet book (preparing for the course) when a guy approached me and asked where I purchased the book from. I noticed he had a Dutch accent, so I made a connection with him. His name was Rene Weisman. He was about my age, thirty, and worked for a rug wholesaler in Holland.

He told me to cancel my taxi; his agent was picking him up to take him to the rug villages and that I was welcome to join them. His agent was the number one rug agent in the area at that time and helped me enormously in finding the stock and suppliers I was hoping for. I was one of the first, if not the first, retailer in the world to go to the villages and buy direct as the manufacturers were all dealing only with carpet wholesalers from around the world. Through this agent's good heart and insistence, the suppliers assisted me and allowed me to purchase small quantities for my single store.

As the saying goes, 'There is no such thing as a self-made man. We all get help from someone.' That someone's name was Nasrudeen and he became my first and dearest Indian friend. We clicked from the moment we met. He was very slim, only about 160 centimetres tall, and had a brilliant memory. He would always tap the side of his head and call his brain 'the computer'. He had a large network of clients and his brother

Fazlu and his two nephews Ozair and Aezaz assisted him. They also manufactured their own rugs.

Nasrudeen was obviously very busy so I began to work with his nephew Aezaz and he became the one that took me around the villages on my future visits and the one that I corresponded and worked with from then on.

In 1975 I went to India in search of Drugs and I found them! In 1979 I returned to India in search of Rugs and I found them!

PERSIAN AND ORIENTAL RUGS

(ONE-DAY SEMINARS)

SATURDAY MARCH 6th
OR
SUNDAY MARCH 14th

Council of Adult Education

ENROLMENT
PERSIAN RUG SEMINAR

Name ....
Address ....
Telephone:
Business ....
Home ....
I wish to enrol in the Seminar
on ☐ March 6th
   ☐ March 14th
I enclose a cheque for the fee of
☐ $22.00
☐ $15
Payable to C.A.E.

Enquiries:
Contact Creative Arts Department
Council of Adult Education
256 Flinders Street, Melbourne 3000
Phone 652 0611

TUTOR : IAN SWART

Mr. Ian Swart, who will conduct the seminars, is an experienced dealer in Persian rugs and comes from a family who have been involved in the business for three generations. Ian has travelled extensively throughout such countries as Iran, Afghanistan, Turkey, Russia, etc. in order to purchase rugs for his clients. He is currently a feature writer for the 'Age' money guide and has tutored with C.A.E. since 1979.

THE VENUE
250 Dorcas Street, South Melbourne

Formerly the Emerald Hill Theatre and a church hall, 250 Dorcas Street has undertaken a somewhat exotic transformation as a Persian carpet warehouse. Thousands of rugs will be on display for students to browse through and comment on during the seminars. A special feature of the seminar will be an authentic Middle Eastern lunch.

THE SEMINAR

The purpose of the seminar is to educate the public as to the determinants of quality, how to distinguish between the various types of rugs and the guidelines as to price structure. The programme will be varied with lectures, films, slides and discussion.

Aezaz

Nasruddeen

Chapter 23

The main rug-making village where Nasrudeen, Aezaz and their families lived and where most of my suppliers were was called, Bhadohi. It was sixty kilometres away from Varanasi. There were no hotels there, so I needed to stay in Varanasi and take the drive each day to Bhadohi.

India had only two makes of car: the Ambassador, modelled on a 1954 Morris Major, and the Premier Padmini, modelled on a 1960 Fiat 1100 (coincidently, my first car, which I had stuck flowers on). The roads to the rug-making villages were rough and it would take up to two hours to cover the sixty-kilometre journey. The cars were non-airconditioned. It was like sitting in a sweatbox. Opening the windows only let in more heat. There was no bottled water, so I had to travel with a bottle of Thumbs Up (an Indian version of Coca-Cola) or Limca (an Indian lemonade) to try and stay hydrated.

The drive from Varanasi to Bhadohi is an experience one will never forget. It is a fascinating drive through small villages with small shops selling local produce, where you would weave your way passed hundreds of women in colourful saris and men walking along the road or on bicycles, children playing, decorated trucks, cows meandering, goats, chickens, pigs and camels. The rural rugged landscape is dotted with small houses made of cow dung walls and farmers tending to their crops.

I took my brother, Nick on one of my buying trips and the visual experience of this drive is one of his travel highlights but one that he feels gave him grey hair.

Once I arrived at Bhadohi, which was a much larger town than the ones we passed on the drive, I encountered a world of rugs. They were transported on rickshaws, tuk-tuks, bicycles, carts, trucks and even camels. The streets are narrow and winding and as we drove along, lots of rugs were lying in open fields to dry. Nearly every building holds a different manufacturer of rugs. If you removed the cars from the village, you would feel that you have gone back 200 years.

I always laughed as we drove through the main Road of Bhadohi. Nasrudeen would say we were now in 5th Avenue, Bhadohi! It was basically a narrow dirt road swarming with people and small shops selling clothes, local wares, fruit, vegetables and bales of wool.

There are two other main rug-making towns: Khamaria and Mirzapur. The drive to these towns is similar to Bhadohi. I have worked in these villages many times but most of my suppliers have been and still are in the Bhadohi region.

Chapter 24

Heading back to Varanasi in 1979 was very different to the trip I had made in 1975 when I first visited there with Ester. The first time, I stayed in the heart of the old city in a budget hotel. This time as I was on a business venture, I stayed at the best hotel in Varanasi at the time called the Varanasi Hotel, several kilometres away from the hustle and bustle of the centre.

I mentioned earlier that the boat ride along the Ganges in Varanasi at sunrise is one of the most amazing experiences one could imagine. I am not an early riser, but I have taken this sunrise boat ride at least thirty times, accompanying family, friends and staff members. I am still fascinated each and every time, having no problem getting up early as I know what is in front of me.

For over 3,000 years, pilgrims from all parts of India have made the journey to the Ganges in Varanasi before sunrise to bathe, drink the holy water, pray, chant and engage in rituals. The scent of incense can become overpowering. Throughout the day, the ghats, which are the steps leading to the river, are a lively hub of activity as people continue to perform religious ceremonies that involve offerings to the river goddess accompanied by traditional music.

Being such a holy city for Hindus, thousands of destitute individuals, mainly elderly, would travel to Varanasi, seeking peace at the end of their lives as this is the holiest place for Hindus to die. There is one pathway along the ghats called Dharmsala where hundreds of poor Indians sit with begging bowls to seek alms and assistance from the visitors and devotees knowing that this is close to the end for them. I have always ensured that I change money into small denominations before heading there and place money in as many of the begging bowls that I can.

The practice of cremations along the Ganges River is rooted in Hindu beliefs. The act of cremating on the ghats and then immersing the ashes into the Ganges is because the Ganges is considered a divine holy river and being cremated there can lead to a more auspicious afterlife.

Timber has always been the traditional way of cremations and every day you will see these burning timber pyre cremations on the ghats, with funeral ceremonies being conducted. Timber has become expensive so now it is only available to the wealthy. Those who didn't have the money to pay were wrapped in white gauze and laid into the river. I have seen many bodies float past me. Since then, they have built gas crematoriums, which many middle-class pay to use as the timber cost is so high. The government uses the gas crematoriums to cremate the poor at government expense so as not to place them in the river.

In the evening, going to the ghats is a different experience. It is much more serene as it is a time for introspection and gratitude. Candlelit lamps are floated down the river as soulful music resonates across the water.

The old walled city of Varanasi is close to the ghats and wandering through the narrow winding streets is like stepping back in time. It is a living museum of Hindu culture and has a feeling of spirituality. On nearly every corner, there seems to be a shrine or a Hindu temple. There are lots of small stores selling trinkets, incense, bracelets and the intricate silk fabrics that Varanasi is famous for. The fabric is known as Benares silk as Benares is the modern British name for Varanasi but now, as with many Indian cities, the names have been changed back to their original Hindu ones. There is a stunning golden temple right in the centre of the old city, which tourists are not permitted to enter but can be viewed for a small fee in a building opposite by climbing its stairs.

The Durga Temple in Varanasi is also known as the Monkey Temple as it is inhabited by a large population of monkeys. As you approach the red-stoned façade, the sound of bells is mixed with the chatter of the monkeys who are climbing the walls and sitting calmly or jumping over carefree, not worrying about the throngs of people entering. There is a large pond next to the temple. The pond has stone stairs at all sides as well as watch towers in the corners. I always love watching the monkeys running up and down those stairs and jumping and diving off the high wall surrounding the pond to cool off.

Sarnath, situated a few kilometres away from the busy centre of Varanasi, is a sacred pilgrimage site for Buddhists. It is the place where Lord Buddha is said to have delivered his first sermon. The Dhamekh Stupa is a massive cylindrical structure with intricate carvings surrounded by beautiful gardens. The Stupa and the peaceful tranquillity of just being there give a calm feeling, inviting visitors to reflect on the teachings of Buddhism. It is a vibrant centre of Buddhism for meditation and prayer and where the teachings of compassion, mindfulness and enlightenment continue.

A cute Varanasi story was told to me: many of the poorer residents of Varanasi have never ventured far from the city. When a small modern shopping centre was built in Varanasi, it had the first-ever escalator in the city, which was a novelty to these residents who had never seen one before. They would bring their children to the shopping centre just to ride up and down on the escalator.

Chapter 25

My ex-wife Ester and her partner Sam were in India at the same time as this first buying trip, having been on an extended trip to India with my beautiful nearly three-year-old daughter. I missed Becky terribly. As they had been away for a couple of months, I decided that it was now my time to be with Becky so I arranged to meet them and bring my daughter home. Fortunately, there was no argument. They were in Manali, which is in the State of Himachal Pradesh in northern India at the end of the Kullu Valley, approximately 2,000 metres high.

It was a long way from where I was in Varanasi. I needed to fly back to Delhi and then catch a six-hour steam train ride to Chandigarh. From Chandigarh, I caught a bus north to Manali, which took another eight hours, up the mountain on a continuous winding road. It was an extremely long uncomfortable journey but it was the only way I could get there and I was prepared to go anywhere to be with my precious daughter.

As the bus was entering the Kullu Valley, I saw fields upon fields of marijuana plants growing. I had to look a few times as I couldn't quite believe what I was seeing. Huge plants were lining both sides of the road.

Manali was a cannabis centre. It was available everywhere, being sold in all sorts of quantities, with hashish also in abundance as Manali hash was well known to be among the best. The only tourists there were either hippies or drug dealers.

Small boys were walking the streets rubbing cannabis buds together in their hands, which is the simplest way of making hashish, and offering it for sale.

Manali was a relatively small hill station. The views were spectacular with snow-capped Himalayan Mountain peaks in the distance, lush green valleys and dense forests. The Kullu people who resided there wore traditional costumes. The women wore long dresses made of wool called 'Pattoo', adorned with intricate geometric or floral patterns and lots of silver jewellery. The men wore knee-length woollen coats called a 'Chola' and a hat that was called a 'Pattu Topi'.

The buildings were generally multi-storeyed. They were built of wood with pagoda-styled sloping roofs and adorned with intricately carved wooden façades.

The only accommodations available were simple guesthouses. I found a small room for myself and as soon as I was settled, I walked through the narrow lanes that were the only roads in the town to the address that Ester had given me.

My meeting with Ester was not particularly comfortable and far from warm but I had to hold back the tears of joy when Becky spotted me and ran into my arms calling, 'Daddy, daddy.' She didn't want to let me go. Tears were now running down my cheeks, but I assured her that I was not going anywhere and that she would be coming home with me very soon.

She remained with Ester and I stayed in Manali for a couple of days, basically stoned the whole time before picking Becky up and beginning the journey back down the mountain in a bus.

It was a very winding road and Becky vomited all over the man sitting in front of us. They had to stop the bus to let Becky out for further vomiting and I had to wipe the poor man's back and shoulder, which was not the most pleasant experience.

After the long journey, we finally arrived in Delhi and went to the Imperial Hotel on Janpath near the Tibetan Market. This hotel had a distinctive Colonial architecture which was a blend of British Colonial and Indian design. It was a stunning timeless example of its time. In 1979, it hadn't been renovated and was relatively inexpensive. The rooms were spacious and, although a little bit dusty, were furnished with stylish Colonial and Indian furnishings.

Even though it was inexpensive, the caste system was quite evident. You would have three different servants looking after your room. There was the higher caste man in a white uniform who would be the one you called for room service or attending to the room. He would take the order and then the one in the khaki uniform would bring the order to you and would also tidy your room. Then there was the lower caste attendant, the untouchable who was on bathroom duty, cleaning the toilets, etc. These three-tiered systems have all but disappeared.

I loved the coffee shop where we ate our meals. It was called the Garden Cottage and the waiters wore white uniforms, sometimes a bit off-white, with turbans and a long red wide ribbon hanging down the back.

Another thing I loved was the Imperial Hotel's beautiful large deco-style swimming pool. That was until I encountered one of the scariest moments of my life.

We were swimming in the pool, having the best time as I threw Becky in the air she would laugh as I caught her. As we were about to leave the pool, I threw her up to let her out. There was a wide lip along the edge of the pool that I wasn't fully aware of and as I strongly threw her up, her head slammed under the lip. She screamed. I freaked out as I thought I had cracked her head open, broken her neck or caused permanent damage. To my relief, of course, she was fine once the crying stopped.

This incident has remained with me forever and whenever I have been in swimming pools with my other children, I always check the lip.

From Delhi, Becky and I flew home to Australia.

Chapter 26

The rugs that Nasrudeen assisted me with on this first buying trip to India for the Persian Carpet Warehouse were a success and as I was now buying direct and shipping from India, not Europe, our margin was greatly improved. I found a variety that I felt was more suitable to the Australian market than those that we purchased in Amsterdam.

European taste was different to ours. Persian carpets have been very popular in Europe for several generations, often being handed down from parents to children. Europeans were very used to having Persian carpets in their homes and the styles that they had always liked and still did, at this time, were very traditional mainly in reds and blues. This was probably also reflected in the climate as it would warm up the room.

Australia was a newer market, a warm country with a more relaxed lifestyle. I could see that consumers preferred softer and more relaxed designs and colours. This was also the trend in America and suppliers told me from the start that I had American taste. It seemed that the American lifestyle and climate were more attuned to Australia's, so I immediately started following American design trends.

I began travelling to Varanasi every three months, each time purchasing more and developing a range that differed from all my competitors. I asked Aezaz to introduce me to at least two new manufacturers each time I visited. I worked hard at building strong relationships with them, gaining their trust and their friendship.

In these early days, Nasrudeen and some of his friends would come in the evening to my hotel room in Varanasi. I always brought two bottles of Johnny Walker Black duty-free with me. They would pour themselves whiskeys, adding lots of water. We ordered snacks, chilli chicken, chicken tikka and pakoras. They smoked like chimneys and some of them couldn't hold their liquor so they would stagger out. I think I would cough myself to sleep due to the fog of smoke and tobacco smell in the room!

The electricity supply in Varanasi was and still is not sufficient to keep the lights on throughout the entire city. Often, it would just turn off without notice so I would be sitting in the room with Nasrudeen and his crew for several minutes in complete darkness speaking as though nothing was different until the hotel generator kicked in. It felt natural and part of everyday life in Varanasi.

Nasrudeen had a magnetic personality. He was loved by all and had lots of friends.

One of these men was called Rai. He was not in the rug business, lived in Bhadohi and was just a fun guy to have around. He worked for Indian Airlines at Varanasi airport and became the Indian Airlines manager. Whenever he saw me arrive at the airport (and still to this day), he would greet me.

Whenever I departed from Varanasi, I always went to his office to say goodbye. He got very excited to see me and called over everyone in the airline office, explaining how I was his old, old friend that he had known for over forty years. If I flew on Indian Airlines, he upgraded me. He recently retired so I will miss our encounters.

Nasrudeen also had lots of contacts and friends in Delhi and we spent lots of time together there where he had an apartment for his second wife who lived in Delhi. Being Muslim, he was permitted more than one wife.

One contact in Delhi was a man who worked for customs. Nasrudeen used to give him backsheesh money to look after his clients. So for many years, whenever I went to leave from Delhi Airport, this man would meet me, take me to the front of the long line, through customs and straight through security.

Chapter 27

Our business was small and these regular trips were quite costly so I would do a scam that would pay for my airfare and more. Overseas products such as video recorders and cameras were not available in India due to import restrictions but were in high demand on the black market. I would buy one duty-free before leaving, remove it from the box and place it in my hand baggage. I was never searched by Indian customs. I must look honest! On arrival in Delhi, I would go to the Palika Bazaar in central Delhi, which is an underground market selling clothes, fabrics, toys and lots of electrical goods including cassettes and DVDs. It wasn't legal for them to be sold but the government turned a blind eye to the goings-on. I would sell my video recorder or camera for double and use the rupees I received in payment to purchase a couple of small silk carpets, carry them home in a suitcase and sell them in the store, making a healthy profit.

Once the economy opened and imported products became available, this scam ended; however, the black market for US dollars was very strong so I would carry US dollars with me from Australia, change them on the black market (where you would get up to thirty per cent more rupees) and use this cash to buy silk carpets and carry them home in my suitcase.

The few that I carried home in my suitcase would tend to sell immediately. They were a beautiful silk product and more affordable than the Persian ones that we stocked at the Persian Carpet Warehouse. I also realised that no other carpet store in Australia stocked them, so I decided to visit Kashmir to purchase a collection. Nasrudeen knew of a manufacturer in Srinagar and referred me to him.

I flew from Delhi to Srinagar in 1981 and purchased a lovely collection from a company called Mirza. They sold well and so I added this to my India trips but as they were not a huge seller due to the price I would visit there once or twice a year.

Chapter 28

On the fourth of November 1979, a group of Iranian militants stormed the US Embassy in Iran, taking fifty-two American diplomats and citizens hostage. The country was now under the rule of Ayatollah Khomeini, a religious leader who had returned Iran to strict Muslim rule. The captors viewed the embassy as a symbol of American interference in their internal affairs. In April 1980, there was a failed military rescue mission. The hostages were finally freed by another attempt by the US in 1981 after 444 days in captivity.

In April 1980, the Australian government banned all trade with Iran except for food and medicine. In September 1980, Iraq invaded Iran and the Iraq-Iran war began, which lasted for eight years.

We saw this as a great selling opportunity for the Persian Carpet Warehouse. Persian rugs were deemed to be an investment as they were the original creators of rugs and due to the embargo on imports from Iran, Persian rugs would be in short supply.

We held our first sale, advertising quite heavily in the newspapers. We were the first rug store to advertise a large sale of Persian rugs from a store in Melbourne. The theme of our sale was centred around the war, hostages, the banning of all trade with Iran and how Persian rugs would be difficult to obtain in the future and would be a great investment. On the first Saturday of our advertising, we opened the doors and were shocked at how busy we were. People were pouring in from everywhere, in search of a bargain! We had a salesman, Phil, working for us and by the end of the day the three of us were worn out, but we had taken more money than we ever dreamed of, so this lifted us from tiredness. The same happened on the following Sunday.

We prepared ourselves for the next weekend, hired my friend Carl again who helped me in the dying days of my father's store and a couple of students to do the flipping and carrying of rugs. We were even busier the second weekend, so we kept advertising and after six weeks, we were all so exhausted that we pulled the plug, intending to hold the same type of sale after a few months of regaining our strength.

We were so wrong! It never got repeated; the momentum had gone and we couldn't revive it.

In those early days, people would enter the store and ask which Persian rugs were the best investment and, in all honesty, I would show them the ones I thought best and would even offer to buy them back at the same price they paid anytime in the future. I honestly believed this to be true.

How wrong I was! The demand for traditional Persian rugs began to decline as years went on and instead of increasing in value, they devalued and are now less expensive than they were many years ago.

Chapter 29

The 1980s was a period with a significant surge in demand for Persian and Oriental rugs in Australia. I mentioned earlier that there was a trend in period homes to remove the wall-to-wall carpeting and polish the floorboards. Now there was also a move to build new homes with hard flooring such as floorboards, terracotta tiling, cork flooring, porcelain tiling, marble, granite or concrete flooring, restricting wall-to-wall carpeting to bedrooms. This remains in vogue today.

The first company to capitalise on this increase in the demand for rugs was Chaudhary's Carpet Palace, a store on High Street, Armadale, owned by Shahid Chaudhary. Shahid was a marketing genius. He took a large risk and advertised massive clearance sales with huge discounts at his store. He placed several full-page advertisements in *The Age* and *Herald Sun,* initiating queues of customers lining outside his store. He would have a security guard at the door and place dummy customers in the queue. This caused the line to be longer. These paid people would enter the store, walk out with a rug, go around the corner, return the rug to the store and go back and stand in line, renewing the process. Traffic would drive by, see the long queue and for fear of missing out, customers would pull over and join the line.

The success of this form of marketing widened and Chaudhary began holding these sales at much larger venues, such as the World Trade Centre, and spread the sales throughout Australia with massive advertising in newspapers Australia-wide. He would offer up to a ninety per cent discount and the public believed it. What he was really doing was marking up his product by 1000% and then offering the discount of ninety per cent, still making a substantial profit.

A second company called Maharajah Carpets soon copied him, as did other dealers, holding massive sales at the showgrounds. They falsely called them 'closing down sales' and handed out false 'made in Iran' certificates for rugs that were actually made in Pakistan.

This caused issues with the genuine rug retailers throughout Australia and we all got together to discuss how to counter these bogus sales. It was obviously affecting us and we contacted consumer affairs and the ACCC. I personally appeared on *A Current Affair* on two occasions to dispute their genuineness. I showed an example of a rug that they advertised at $80,000 reduced to $8,000. The rug in question was a fine-quality Pakistan rug of which I had the same rug in stock. My retail price was $8,000.

The ACCC finally took action and several of these companies were fined for false and misleading conduct. These bogus sales finally ended.

It caused issues with us in that we were losing sales to these events. We were continually asked when we were going on sale or when we were having a closing-down sale and everyone bargained with us, expecting a massive discount.

There was a comedy show at the time called *Fast Forward*. Steve Vizard and Peter Moon, two well-known TV celebrities, made fun of these bogus sales with a weekly segment on the show where they acted as Pakistani rug salesmen and made a farce offering massive discounts on their 'fokhari' rugs.

This negative response we received at first benefited us greatly in the long term. Due to the massive advertising, newspaper articles discussing the fact that these sales were bogus plus the segments on *Fast Forward*, there was a huge increase in people's awareness of rugs. People wanted a rug in their homes and would now seek out genuine rug companies.

Chapter 30

In chapter one, I mentioned that my father had one second cousin, a small boy who survived the Holocaust. His name is Sam Wennek.

During the Holocaust, he was among the 500+ children rescued by the Dutch underground from a daycare centre near the Hollandsche Schouwburg. From July 1943 to May 1945, he was hidden by several families, often transferred through safe houses in Amsterdam. After the war, his uncle, who had migrated to the USA before the war, arranged for him to go to New York. Three months later, he was sent to Australia where his aunt, my father's cousin, adopted him and raised him in Australia. He attended Scots College in Queensland and as an adult in 1960, he returned to the Netherlands.

In 1962, Sam was assisting an Oriental carpet dealer from South Africa based in London, specialising in the sale of Persian carpets through exhibitions and auctions. In 1969, he acquired Rippon Boswell, a renowned UK antique rug auction company.

Sam opened a rug store in London and also in Zurich, which is where he currently resides. Two of his sons work with him in the business.

How amazing is that my only living relative of my father's family is also in the Persian carpet business!

So, my father, Sam, my maternal grandparents and Uncle Coenie have all been involved in the carpet industry. It obviously runs through my veins!

Sam is ten years older than me, and I don't remember meeting him in Australia while growing up but I looked him up when I first visited Europe.

He held an auction of antique carpets in Australia in 1980 and contacted Coenie and me at the Persian Carpet Warehouse as he had heard we had opened a store together. His auction did not go well as antique carpets were not appreciated in Australia at that time, unlike in Europe. He offered to leave the stock with us on consignment and we held onto them for about a year, selling only one and sending the balance back to Europe.

After sending the stock back, he said to us that doing business together was like having a birthday: 'Many happy returns!'

We never did business together again, but I told Sam of my relationship with Nasrudeen and the next time Sam went to Varanasi, he looked him up and was equally impressed by Nasrudeen's ability and contacts so he took him on as his Indian agent.

As we now had a mutual contact in India, on occasion we happened to be in Varanasi at the same time, so we spent time together. As Nasrudeen's family was large, there were many wedding celebrations in Bhadohi and Sam and I attended several of these together.

Muslim village marriages are mostly arranged where a family member, a close friend or a third person helps bring two compatible people together. The bride and groom have usually never met before but have several 'meet and greet' opportunities, allowing them to gain a sense of familiarity before marriage.

I asked Aezaz why many arranged marriages are successful and in simple terms, he told me that children have respect for their parents and believe that parents know what is best for their child. The parents have gone to lengths to find the right match, so the bride and groom have a commitment to making it work. Whilst the relationship may not focus on romantic love initially, the couples grow close, love and romance following.

The *nikah* is the formal marriage ceremony performed by an Islamic cleric usually at a mosque where the bride and groom exchange vows. The *walima* is the formal reception hosted by the husband and wife.

Traditionally, a Muslim wedding reception in an Indian village brings together neighbours, friends and relatives to enjoy the religious rituals and traditional festivities.

These receptions were large, with up to 2,000 guests from the village and held in a large outdoor fenced-off area. The bride and groom sit at the entrance, greeting the guests who then enter the appropriate side as the sexes are segregated. A temporary petition, usually made from a fabric known as 'pardah', creates a physical barrier between men and women, upholding the traditional principles of modesty. This allows women to participate in the ceremony without being visible to men.

There is a lavish feast with huge pots of traditional Indian dishes being served such as various curries, biryani, kebabs, korma and Indian sweets. Alcohol is not served and traditional music is played throughout the evening.

Somayya & Abdul Mahbood

Aezaz, daughter, wife at daughters wedding

Chapter 31

In 1978, the People's Democratic Party of Afghanistan (PDPA) established a socialist government in Afghanistan following a coup. The Soviet Union (Russia), being a socialist state, supported the PDPA but was concerned by the spread of Islamic fundamentalism in Afghanistan and in the Central Asian republics of the Soviet Union, which had significant Muslim populations. They also wanted to counter the perceived threat from the United States as Afghanistan was strategically important by providing access to the Persian Gulf so in December of 1979, they invaded Afghanistan and immediately took complete military and political control of Kabul and large portions of the country. I travelled to Kabul in 1980 and couldn't believe how this peaceful country that I had visited twice before was now under strict military control. Wherever I went, I would be stopped by Soviet soldiers, questioned and had to show my passport. I didn't feel safe and have not travelled to Afghanistan since.

Many of the carpet dealers and other Afghans left Afghanistan by escaping across the border, living in Peshawar Pakistan in refugee camps. The carpet dealers moved on to Karachi and Lahore to sell their carpets, which were being smuggled out of Afghanistan. I had been told of this, so I decided to travel to Karachi in search of Afghan carpets and was also interested in purchasing Pakistani Bokharas, which were popular at the time.

So, in 1981, I went to Karachi to buy rugs for the Persian Carpet Warehouse. I had been referred to an agent who was an Afghani Jew. Excited that I, too, was Jewish, he invited me to his home for Shabbat dinner. His wife and nine children had emigrated to Israel as life was not easy being Jewish in Muslim Pakistan. He had a Eunuch house boy who cooked us a delicious kosher shabbat meal after which he did an exotic dance for us. Boy, was that a weird experience!

The agent asked me to please join him at the synagogue the next morning, being the Sabbath. He picked me up at my hotel and we started walking. It was 'Eid al-Fitr', the festival of breaking the fast, the end of Ramadan. The streets were lined with Muslims on their prayer rugs, all wearing white, chanting and praying. It was quie surreal, walking through the crowds of Muslims as we made our way to the synagogue.

It was called the Magain Shalome Synagogue and was built in 1893. There was only a small Jewish community in Karachi but they opened a Hebrew school at the synagogue premises and the community were quite observant. In 1948, once the partition of British India had occurred and Pakistan became a Muslim majority, the synagogue was set on fire. Jews all over Pakistan were attacked so many of them fled to Hindu India for safety. After each of the Arab-Israeli wars, the frequency of attacks on Jews increased so by the mid-1970s, most of the Jews from Pakistan had migrated to Israel. There were only six members of the congregation remaining when I visited the synagogue on that day. As they had no Rabbi, each took turns at conducting the service. They were so happy to have a Jewish guest from Australia attend a Shabbat service and kept referring to me by my Hebrew name, Yitzhak ben Levi. Soon after, my Afghan agent also emigrated to Israel. On the 17th of July 1988, the synagogue was demolished and a shopping mall was built in its place.

My Jewish-Afghan agent introduced me to Afghan refugee carpet dealers. They conducted their business in old apartment buildings with rooms full of Afghan rugs. One would enter these musty old apartments, devoid of furniture, to find the Afghanis sitting, sleeping and eating on the piles of carpets. The apartments didn't have proper kitchens but in the corner would be a small fridge and a small portable stove for cooking and making tea. The men would often be sitting around in their traditional clothing and turbans, at times, smoking a shisha pipe.

My Afghan agent also introduced me to a few Pakistani carpet manufacturers but not long after, the Afghan agent left Pakistan and moved to Israel. One of the Pakistani carpet manufacturers was called Tariq. I trusted him so Tariq would take me to the apartment buildings and translate for me as I sifted through and selected extremely dusty rugs. My eyes turned red and burned from the dust flying around as they opened them up for me. He collated the rugs from the various apartments, paid them on charge to me and arranged to ship them to Australia with the Pakistani carpets that I purchased from him.

I would regularly be invited to Tariq's home for dinner. Alcohol was strictly banned in Pakistan so Tariq would carefully close all the curtains and produce a bottle of whiskey to share before sitting down for our meal. His servants, under the direction of his wife, would prepare a traditional dish of chicken or lamb curry served with fragrant basmati rice followed usually by Gulab Jamun, which is a sweet dumpling in syrup.

On my first visit to Karachi, I showed my press pass upon checking in at the Hilton Hotel. I had a fake Dutch press pass, which a friend in Holland arranged for me, and I would often show it to check in to hotels as it often provided me a discount or an upgrade. It made me feel very special, being a part of the international press!

It impressed the Hilton staff and they did give me a discount but the next morning, the police knocked on my door asking what a member of the Dutch press was doing in Pakistan. I was shaking inside but somehow talked my way out, explaining that I was writing an article for a Dutch newspaper on the making of hand-made rugs in Pakistan. Fortunately, I was carrying a couple of rug books with me, which I showed them. They believed me and left. After that incident, I never used my press pass again on my travels!

The press pass, however, became useful to me in Australia. I would show it at the Australian Open Tennis, which allowed me access; however, this was stopped after a few years. At the Waverley Football Ground where my football team the St Kilda Football Club played its home games, I would show the pass each week at the parking entrance, would not be charged the parking fee and would be guided to the press area right at the entrance to the ground. This worked for many years.

I often had a friend Russell and his children in the car with me. Russell noticed how they didn't really study the press pass but would wave me through when I flashed it and called out 'press'. One time, when he wasn't with us, Russell flashed his library card, called out 'press' 'and they waved him through.

Chapter 32

In 1982 I started dating my second and current wife, Gina. We had been dating for about six weeks when Gina's father, a well-renowned Melbourne architect, asked her older sister Sandra what I was like. I had known her sister Sandra and her husband Rodney for many years as they were a similar age to me. Sandra replied to her father that at the previous Christmas, we were staying at the same hotel on the Gold Coast and that I was a lovely guy with a beautiful little daughter.

To say this shocked him would be an understatement. He later called Gina aside and told her that she was forbidden to go out with me. He screamed in no mild manner that I was fifty per cent older than her (I was thirty-two, she was twenty-one), that she would be a second-hand rose as I was a divorced man with a child, I was a rug gypsy and that I lived in a house made of sticks (I had recently moved into an Edwardian weatherboard house in Malvern).

This outburst by her father totally backfired. She packed her bags, moved out of her parent's home moved into mine, not speaking to her father for the next two years.

It was a shock to me. I probably wasn't ready for her to move in, but I must say we were falling in love and it certainly worked out.

Over time, her father's attitude towards me changed and later he showed a lot of respect for the way I looked after Gina, Becky and the three children we had together: Dan, who was born in 1987, Sophie in 1989 and Elijah in 1993 (whom we usually refer to as Eli). Being an architect and an avid furniture and art collector, he also showed interest in the rugs that I was importing and had admiration for the way I conducted my business.

Chapter 33

A successful retail store is dependent upon finding the best location. I always believed that the best place in Melbourne to have a rug store was High Street, Armadale and was quite determined to open a store there. Rents were very high in High Street and my uncle wasn't prepared at his age to take risks. He was content with the store we had together in South Melbourne and his store at the Southern Cross.

I opened the first Hali rug store in 1982 on the corner of High St and Stuart Street in a beautiful large building. I needed a partner so my cousin Theo, with whom I had travelled to Ootacamund, teamed up with me. The name Hali was chosen as the number one rug magazine in the world was called Hali. We liked the name but didn't know what it meant. Later, we got to know that the word 'Hali' is the Turkish and Greek word for carpet.

It was a big risk opening on High Street as the store was large, in the best part of the street and the rent was very high, but I was prepared to go for it as I was full of confidence. It was going to succeed. I remember two of my competitors entering the store and telling me that I would fail within six months as there would be no way I could make enough to pay the rent. Those two competitors are still in the industry and each still has the one, original store.

The demands of the public were changing. Interior designers wanted the rug to match the colours of their client's room and furniture and as I mentioned earlier, hard flooring was now very much in vogue. They were seeking decoration on the floor, colour being the number one element.

More people were asking for modern rugs of which there were very few in Australia.

Through my experience in the rag trade, I knew I had a good knowledge of fashion, colour and Australian taste and as the key element to building a successful retail business is in the buying, this was my competitive advantage. Luck was with me as all my competitors were Persian or Pakistani and even though they had great knowledge of handmade rugs, they weren't in tune with the Australian taste that I had. Something I took great advantage of.

I heard that the most successful modern rug manufacturer in all of India was called Shyam Ahuja. His showroom was in Bombay so before opening the High Street store, I decided to go to Bombay and visit him.

I met Shyam at his beautiful modern showroom in Worli, a suburb of Bombay. He was a most impressive upper-class Indian gentleman, oozing with charm and taste. People often referred to him as the Ralph Lauren of India! After describing my new store and the vision I had moving forward, he agreed to sell me his products to Hali on an exclusive basis for Australia.

Shyam Ahuja is known to have re-invented the traditional Indian dhurrie. An Indian dhurrie is a flat woven rug that has been part of Indian culture for centuries. They are traditional in design and colour but were no longer in demand in Western countries.

Shyam introduced contemporary designs and colours into dhurries while still handweaving them in the traditional way. They were beautiful and Shyam was successful in selling them worldwide, particularly in the USA.

His range also consisted of modern hand-tufted carpets, more intricate modern hand-knotted carpets and a stunning range of handwoven cushions.

I was instantly drawn to all his products so I decided to purchase his full collection and dedicate a large area of the store solely to Shyam

Ahuja as I knew this look, never seen in Australia before, would gain a lot of attention.

The High Street store was a large double-fronted building, so we dedicated the right-hand side window and section behind to Shyam Ahuja by branding his name on the window, creating a store within a store. We established a strong bond with Shyam and he and his wife visited us on two occasions in Australia. His son, Vikram, and wife, Mirra, worked in Shyam's business so I met with them on a regular basis and would often spend evenings with them in Bombay.

I was the first person to introduce modern handmade rugs and dhurries to Australia.

In the larger part of the store, we stocked traditional rugs from India, Iran, Caucasia, Turkey and Afghanistan as at that time the traditional rugs were still the majority of our sales.

I took a leaf out of Shyam's book and got creative. I altered the colours of the Indian traditional hand-knotted rugs made in Bhadohi to more modern colours that suited Australian taste. It proved to be extremely successful. I would sit on traditional rugs in Bhadohi with wool balls and indicate to my suppliers which colours to change to more modern pastel or muted tones. I introduced variations of the colour green into the rugs, a colour on trend at the time but traditionally, green was rarely used in rugs as green is considered a sacred colour in the Muslim faith. It is believed that the prophet Mohammed wore a green cloak and that it would be sacrilege to walk over it. My suppliers were intrigued by what I was doing and would sample pieces for me, which I would then view on my next visit and either approve or make further adjustments. These Indian traditional rugs that I introduced in modern colours became more and more in demand in Australia as did the demand for our modern Shyam Ahuja rugs.

The first day that we opened Hali was a Saturday and I was rostered on in South Melbourne so Gina went to assist Theo if they became busy.

From the moment the door opened, they were flat out. People were curious as no one had seen a rug store like it with its modern touch. My uncle dropped in with a bottle of champagne to wish us good luck but it was so busy that neither Theo nor Gina could stop to talk to him. The store became busier and busier and its success caused friction between my uncle and myself. As Hali was doing better and better, I was spending less time in South Melbourne. I could see a much greater growth potential in my newer venture so in late 1984, about two years after opening Hali, I sold my share in the Persian Carpet Warehouse to my uncle.

Chapter 34

The first ever All India Carpet Fair was held in Varanasi at the Varanasi Hotel in 1982. I attended this first fair with Nasrudeen's clients from around the world. There were eleven of us and Nasrudeen organised a large dinner with Indian music and dancing girls. It was a wonderful night and the first time I got to meet buyers from Germany, Holland, Spain, Brazil and America.

As I wandered around the fair, I visited many stalls of rug producers and found two new suppliers of note.

Badrudeen Ansari had a stunning collection of fine quality traditional rugs in beautiful, harmonised colours and a collection of Mir carpets (a paisley repeating design rug), a popular rug that he produced in a multitude of colours. He was a master in the industry and for many years became my major supplier. I introduced two versions of Green Mirs to him, which he also began selling to other clients around the world. From then on, he referred to me as Mr Green. Sadly, he passed away about fifteen years ago so his son Naseem took over the business and by terrible misfortune, during Covid, Naseem, his wife and mother all died from the virus, closing the business.

My second new supplier was Ramesh Baranwal. He produced a mid-quality handmade rug, had good colour sense and I worked with him, designing and colouring rugs for many years. After he passed away, his three sons took over the business and Hali still works with them.

Both of these gentlemen and I formed a lovely relationship. I was very sad when they passed away.

I was the first Australian to attend this fair and would endeavor to attend each year, often finding something new suppliers and products.

Shortly after opening Hali, we employed a salesman to assist us as it was too busy for the two of us to handle alone. His name was David Pickard and David remained a loyal employee for forty years until he retired. We are still close friends.

In 1984, I attended the fair again and took David along so that he could expand his knowledge of the industry and see first-hand the making of rugs. Being the only Australian there, I was asked to give a speech about the Indian carpet industry and my thoughts on how it should improve. I do remember that the speech was well received but to be honest, I can't really remember what I said possibly because of the following:

Indian whiskey is very harsh and strong and that is what was offered at the evening meetings of the fair. I obviously drank to excess and became very drunk. We shared a room and the morning after, I awoke lifted my head, looked at David and said, 'Oh no.' I went back to sleep, remaining in bed the entire day to recover. A day of work lost.

Chapter 35

As mentioned previously, the mainstay of the rug business at this time consisted of selling traditional rugs so besides those that I was purchasing in India, I also required Persian, Turkish, Afghan and Caucasian rugs. I continued dealing with Kelaty in London, which, as explained earlier, was the largest wholesaler of handmade rugs in the world, based in London.

The Kelaty family were one of the nicest genuine families I ever had the pleasure of knowing. Levi Kelaty was the founder. He was born in Bombay of Persian descent and a religious Jew. He emigrated to London in 1953 and began trading in rugs. He visited the USSR several times and eventually got the exclusive rights to the beautiful handmade rugs that were being made in Kazak, Sirvan and Azerbaijan. He built up a massive business with rugs from all the rug-making countries. His warehouse was huge, and it is reputed that at one stage he had 100,000,000 pounds of stock. He was a gentleman and always wore his hat even when he flipped stacks himself, never allowing his customers to help. There were, of course, many staff moving rugs everywhere as they had a huge client base selling to all the world and had clients every day.

Levi told me a story once about having rugs made in China, the country that was able to reproduce items perfectly. He handed his supplier a small Persian prayer rug and asked him to produce 100 pieces. The original piece had a small ungainly kink along the side. The Chinese made 100 pieces all with the same kink.

His three sons, David, Michael and Danny were all in their early twenties when I started working with them and his daughter Elizabeth worked in the office. At one p.m., a bell would ring for lunch. The buyers, and there were always several in the building at the same time, would go to the dining room, and all sit with Levi and his family to a beautifully prepared lunch made by Mrs Lillian Kelaty herself.

Levi looked much older than he was; in fact, I thought he was about seventy but in 1987, he passed away at age fifty-seven. Sadly, his beautiful daughter Elizabeth passed away soon after.

The lunches continued after his death and his eldest son, David, who was still in his twenties, took over the company and we became very close friends. He was single and took me to exclusive clubs in London. We had dinner together and I sometimes stayed with him at his beautiful two-storey apartment off Oxford Street near Selfridges. When Becky went on her extended trip overseas at age twenty-one, she stayed at David's apartment for about ten weeks.

These trips to London often coincided with my trips to India. In my early days of buying in India, I would sometimes buy hashish and smoke in my hotel room in Delhi. On one of my trips to London to visit Kelaty after being in India, I was walking through the green zone at Heathrow Airport when they stopped me and asked me to open my suitcase. One customs officer went off with my passport and Swiss army knife while the other searched my suitcase.

The officer came back with a piece of litmus paper that had a brownish/yellow mark on it. He told me that this was a smear of cannabis resin, so they took me with my suitcase to another room. I told them that as it was freely available in India, I thought I would try it and use my knife to cut it but I wasn't carrying any and I am not a dealer, which of course I wasn't. They made me strip, which was very humiliating. They looked under my feet and between my legs but fortunately, no internal. My suitcase was gone through with a fine-tooth comb. I remember how carefully they checked the lining of the suitcase and of my jackets. Naturally, nothing was discovered so they let me into London.

Chapter 36

It was a joy for me to travel to London as I still loved fashion and would always buy my clothes when visiting London. It was more fun than buying at home plus there was a much greater choice as well as being a season ahead.

I have always been into trendy shirts. In the early eighties, I discovered a small shop in Covent Garden called Ted Baker. There was a middle-aged lady working there and as I looked through the rack of shirts, she asked me which clothing company I worked for. I told her I didn't, but she answered with, 'Yes, you do. I can tell from the way you are examining the shirts.' I explained that I was in the rug trade not the rag trade but that my training was in the rag trade and hence I had a certain way of viewing fashion as I used to look through the racks when selecting samples.

This was Ted Baker's first store and the lady turned out to be Ted Baker's mother. Mrs Baker was very proud of her 'Teddy'. Later they opened a store within Harrods and Mrs Baker moved there. I would visit her each time in London when buying my shirts, always laughing over our first meeting. The Ted Baker label became huge, becoming a public company with stores in most major cities of the world.

I still love and buy Ted Baker shirts!

Chapter 37

In 1984, Hali's Persian stock was running low so I needed to make a trip to London to purchase stock from Kelaty.

Gina was a primary school teacher so we coincided with the mid-year school holidays and went for a three-week trip to London and Europe, having a break together and I could purchase the rugs I needed. I asked her where else she would like to go besides London and she suggested Paris as she loved style and had fond memories of the fashionable, romantic, artistic, historical city that it was from her memory of travelling there with her family when she was a young girl.

On the Metro in Paris, we were sitting on the small flip seats at the end of the carriage. As we were pulling into a station, I told her this was where we got off and stood up, realising it wasn't and sat back down. Gina also stood up; her flip seat did too. Gina sat back down straight on the floor. The entire carriage laughed in unison!

After a few glorious days visiting the sights of Paris, we decided to explore more. We were sitting in our cute small left-bank hotel, trying to decide where to go next as we hadn't really planned our movements or research. We opened a map of Europe in front of us on the bed and I turned to Gina and suggested maybe Madrid in Spain. Gina looked up at me and said, 'When do we leave?' Within minutes, we walked to the station to arrange tickets for the next day.

The station was packed with people commuting home from work and we struggled to find the ticket office as we pushed our way through the crowds. We bought tickets for the train leaving the next evening for Madrid and were informed that as it was a Spanish train, it followed strict Catholic rules. Therefore, as we weren't married, we couldn't sleep in the same compartment, so Gina joined three ladies in one and I with three men in another. We handed our passports to the train conductor as we would be crossing the border overnight. At three a.m., we were each woken up at the border, taken out of our cabins and told to get off the train as we foolishly didn't realise we needed visas.

There we were at the station in Perpignan, which was the border town, in the middle of the night looking at each other like, 'What have we done? What fools. What do we do now?' We walked into town carrying our suitcases (they hadn't invented wheels for suitcases in the 1980s) and found a lovely small boutique-style hotel. We knocked and banged on the door at 3.30 a.m. and saw the angry face of someone whose sleep had been interrupted as the door opened. Once we explained our situation, he was most hospitable and welcomed us in. The owners and the hotel were charming. We sat in our room and couldn't sleep, pondering where to go next. Realising we needed to stay in France, we got our map out again and this time, Gina said to leave it to her, suggesting we make our way to the French Riviera. After a beautiful French breakfast of fresh camembert and jambon baguettes, we walked back to the station. It was only a small station so this time we had no problem finding the ticket office and were informed that there was a train leaving for Marseilles, the gateway to the Riviera, at midnight. As it was leaving on the same day, we were too late to book reserved seats but were told to not worry but to turn up anyway as there would still be seats available.

We arrived at the station in time and the train pulled in. I placed one suitcase onto the train and it started moving out of the station. We were still on the platform, so Gina jumped on the train to be with her suitcase and I was still standing on the platform with my suitcase. Suddenly, Gina was disappearing as I watched her and the train heading into the distance. I then realised that Gina had my man bag with my passport, cash, cigarettes and credit cards. I thought I should go back to the hotel where I had been as they were so lovely there and would give me a room even though I had no money. Via my limited French, I tried to explain my predicament to people on the platform and was told that the second half of the train was coming in half an hour. Without thinking, I jumped on! No ticket, no cash, no passport, no cigarettes. I begged the conductor to let me ride, botted cigarettes and told the entire train my sob story. Definitely not the best decision as once I got to Marseilles, how would I find Gina? We didn't have mobile phones in those days and had not pre-discussed accommodation, so I had no way to contact her.

After an hour, Gina's train stopped at a very small station. She was told that there would be a train stopping there in a half hour going back to Perpignan so she hopped off, assuming I would go back to the same hotel, which, of course, would have been the smart decision for me. After an hour, my train slowed down and I spotted Gina sitting alone on a small bench in the dark waiting for the train back to Perpignan. The whole train knew my story. I yelled, 'There is my girlfriend,' so nearly the whole train called out in unison, 'Get on the train, get on the train.' Gina ran over the tracks with her suitcase and we were united.

We often think about what would have happened had I not spotted Gina on that bench, and I would have gone to Marseilles without money a credit card or a passport as I had no idea where she would be staying. She wouldn't have waited for me at the station as she probably wouldn't have known that the train had a second half following. Remember, we didn't have mobiles!

We took the same train twenty-four hours later to Marseilles, hopping on the train at the same time each with a suitcase. We weren't going to repeat the experience of the night before!

When we returned to Paris to catch our flight home, we were on the Metro again and as we pulled into a station, I told her this is where we got off. Gina stepped off and the doors closed before I could work my way through the crowd. We had learnt our lesson from the Perpignan experience, so Gina stayed put, I got off at the next station, went back to where the last place we were together and she was waiting for me. I have seen her in much better moods though!

Chapter 38

At the end of that same year, Gina accompanied me on her first trip to India. She had heard me countless times describe Delhi, Agra, Varanasi and Bhadohi and how I had established a network of friends through my business. Now she could experience it for herself. She loved it from the first minute.

Naturally, she had a great guide and we started off in Delhi. I showed her all the sights and we stayed at my favourite hotel, the Imperial.

We caught the train to Agra so Gina could see the splendour of the Taj Mahal. In those years, you were able to walk into the Taj Mahal and touch the walls but in 2018, the Indian government placed a barricade around the interior to stop tourists touching it and causing damage.

Later in the day, close friends of ours from Australia, Debra and Michael, arrived. It was New Year's Eve and also happened to be a full moon. A full moon is the absolute best time to see the Taj Mahal at night as it glistens at its whitest, so we all went back and looked in amazement as it shimmered and shined during a full moon when darkness set in.

Debra and Michael surprised us by producing a small bag of cocaine. I have never been and am not a regular user of the substance but on very special occasions or functions, I do partake. This certainly made the Taj Mahal shimmer even more. To top the night off, we went to a New Year's Eve party at our hotel, the music being played by an Indian Beatles cover band. It was hilarious – my favourite band and here I am forty years later, remembering this fabulous night like it was yesterday.

We parted our friends and went to Varanasi so Gina could finally meet Nasrudeen and some of my other friends and suppliers. As mentioned earlier, Nasrudeen is a very small man and I have a very cute photo of Nasrudeen sitting on Gina's knee.

In Bhadohi, everyone was fascinated by Gina's fair skin and blonde hair. I think at times she felt like she was Princess Diana, the person she was obsessed with, as wherever we went in Bhadohi, people stared at her in fascination. No tourists had ever visited this town, so she was certainly a novelty.

After Bhadohi, I decided that we should go on an adventure to places I hadn't previously visited so we made our way to Jodhpur, which is a beautiful city situated in the southern part of Rajasthan called the 'Blue City' as the buildings in the old quarter are painted blue to keep the interiors cool during the scorching desert heat.

The newer city has interesting architecture with a blend of Indian, British and Art Deco buildings often referred to as 'Indo Deco'. We stayed at the magnificent Umaid Bhawan Palace, which was the last Maharajah Palace to be built in India the building of which commenced in 1929 and was not completed until 1943. It was one of the world's largest private residences when completed but has since been converted into three parts: a hotel, a museum and the current maharajah living in a third section. He proudly walked around the hotel, introducing himself to the guests. Apparently, 2500 people were employed in its construction, which helped to employ drought-stricken farmers during these years. The hotel rooms were stunning, as were the large banquet hall and the magnificent indoor Indo-Deco swimming pool, reminiscent of a movie set in the 1940s with a massive swing that hung from the high ceiling above.

I loved strolling through the bustling bazaar of the old town where they displayed local textiles, handicrafts, spices and traditional Rajasthani food. Overlooking the city perched on a rocky hill was the massive awe-inspiring fort known as the Mehrangarh Fort. The people of Jodhpur are extremely hospitable and it is a city that offers a real taste of Rajasthani's rich and colourful heritage.

We caught the evening overnight train through the desert to Jaisalmer, a city situated on the edge of the Thar Desert near the Pakistan border.

On the train, we were given a 'bed roll', which is like an old-style sleeping bag to sleep in – dusty old thing it was! Jaisalmer is an ancient, fortified city, situated on top of a small mountain made of sandstone with a view overlooking vast and picturesque sand dunes of the Thar Desert. The fort has a myriad of narrow winding streets, centuries-old homes and ornate Jain temples. It was not a tourist destination in those days and was quite primitive. Our hotel didn't have showers, so we washed with buckets that the staff brought to us and filled daily with hot water. A highlight for us was an overnight camel safari. We rode camels into the golden arid desert, exploring the many undulating sand dunes. The sunset was breathtaking and we spent a night under the stars in a traditional desert camp, eating dahl and vegetarian curry with chapatis cooked over an open fire.

From Jaisalmer, we caught a day train to Delhi. We felt very dusty and dirty so I suggested to Gina that we would treat ourselves and stay in a luxury hotel with beautiful hot showers that we were craving for. I had previously driven past a new hotel built for the Asian games called the Kanishka so I suggested that we stay there. No argument from Gina! It had a beautiful marble lobby, and we caught the lift to our floor. The lift was small, the halls were very narrow and the room was not so clean or special but it had a hot shower. Excitedly, I bagged the first shower. I washed my long hair and my body, removed the towel from the rack above and dried myself all over as well as rubbed the towel into my hair to help dry it. To my shock and horror, I looked and saw that someone had wiped their arse with that towel and placed it neatly back on the shelf. Five showers later, I felt clean! I called management up and made them look at and smell the towel. I was naturally upset and angry and from memory, the only compensation I received was a bowl of shrivelled fruit and fresh towels without faeces.

Now you are all victims to my story and will forever check your hotel towels before drying yourselves!

This reminds me of a common thing that would happen to tourists when walking the streets in Delhi or Bombay. A shoeshine boy would ask if you wanted your shoes polished. You would automatically look down and see that one of your shoes would have a streak of dung across it, so of course you would pay to have them cleaned. Another small boy had walked past you just before and without you noticing would smear your shoe with dung. They were in partnership and had a thriving business!

Chapter 39

In 1985, I heard rumours within the industry that there was another up-and-coming trendy rug company making a variety of modern rugs and dhurries called Zeba. I arranged to visit their showroom in Bombay and was introduced to the proprietor a tall handsome Indian man of about the same age as myself who had been educated at a University in England and lived there for a few years after. He spoke in perfect English with a touch of a British accent and had a great sense of humour and a jovial manner. His name is Rajan Mehta and I instantly enjoyed his company. His collection of dhurries, hand-tufted and hand-knotted rugs impressed me greatly so I placed an order with him.

The rugs arrived in Australia several months later and when we unpacked them, Theo turned to me and said, 'If these rugs sell, I will eat my hat.' They sold successfully and we continued a long business relationship. Theo never ate his hat!

From then on, I would travel regularly to Bombay to visit Shyam Ahuja and Zeba.

Rajan's first office was at the famous Wankhede Cricket Stadium. Downstairs, there was a section where private businesses operated. When my friend Michael joined me on an Indian trip, he went upstairs to watch cricket players practising whilst I worked with Rajan downstairs. There was a young boy practising that Michael thought looked outstanding. This boy was sixteen years old and had just been selected for the Indian cricket team. His name was Sachin Tandulkar.

I loved my time with Rajan in Bombay. He became and still is a very good and dear friend of mine even though we haven't conducted business together for several years. He was a member of the Bombay Gymkhana, which was a club that was a relic of the British Raj, now frequented by wealthier Indians. I always accompanied him there and loved the time together. It had a great bar with the best bloody Mary ever, delicious bar snacks, a fabulous restaurant, squash courts, billiard tables, a cricket pitch and tennis courts. The tennis court base was made from pressed cow dung and Rajan and I would play tennis there regularly.

I find it fascinating and charming to walk around the Colaba area of Bombay (now called Mumbai, its origin Indian name), so ever since my first time when visiting Shyam Ahuja I have stayed in Colaba.

I would stay at the Diplomat Hotel, which was a small hotel situated behind the famous five-star Taj Mahal Palace Hotel, which I couldn't afford. The rooms were very basic but did have an ensuite bathroom. The smell of Indian food was everywhere as many of the guests would bring a small portable stove and cook their meals in their room. When you walked along the corridors, there were disused beds piled up to the sides and you would almost have to walk sideways to pass them. Every now and then, a rat would scamper past. Each morning, I would walk over to the Taj Mahal Hotel and eat a delicious breakfast at the beautiful Shamiana Restaurant.

The same man at the Diplomat operated the lift for years. He wore the same size shoe as myself so I would always leave him a pair of shoes. It got to the point that as I so frequently visited this hotel, he would look at my feet when I arrived to see what shoes he would be getting, and I would look down to see if he was wearing the shoes I gave him on the last trip.

Once, I was on a very delayed flight arriving at Bombay around midnight. I don't remember why but for some reason I hadn't booked the Diplomat or any other hotel. I caught a taxi to the Diplomat but there were no rooms. The taxi drove me to every hotel in the Colaba area, but no rooms were available. I finally succumbed to going to the five-star Taj

Mahal Palace Hotel. There was not a room available there either. It was probably two a.m. by then and I didn't know what to do. The staff at the Taj were so kind that they allowed me to sleep on a couch in their lobby. I woke up in the morning to a buzz of people. I jumped up, washed in the communal bathroom and went on my way.

I have taken the drive from Bombay Airport into Colaba so often that I recognised the same beggars at their assigned traffic lights. There were beggars at every intersection. These beggars were mainly controlled by the Indian mafia and were a well-known racket that existed in most major Indian cities on the main arterial roads. Most of the time, they were children, especially little girls or young women holding babies, obviously in ragged clothes and particularly dirty as this received more sympathy from people. They were forced into begging by the mafia, often being stolen from their parents. At the end of the day, they were forced to hand the money over to the handler. Most disturbing was that some of the children were intentionally maimed as this evoked even more sympathy. If they didn't bring in enough income for the mafia, the child was further maimed. Often, when the young girls got a bit older, they sold them to the prostitution industry for a generous sum. Very few Indians give to these beggars on the road and tourists are learning not to in the hope of ending this horrible practice.

There were many other beggars in India sitting on footpaths and I usually gave to those who looked genuine and in need, but it was difficult to know which ones were controlled by the mafia or not.

There were another group of beggars that I often saw on the roads usually, walking in small groups known as the 'hijra'. They were transvestites, transgender, transexuals and eunuchs. These people were ostracised by society due to their gender identity, were very poor and made their living by begging, singing, dancing or prostitution. Moving forward in 2014, they were recognised by the Indian court as a third gender and since then have been much more accepted into society.

One time, two young boys approached my car, asking for rupees, as I was driving to the airport in Mumbai. They didn't look that impoverished and had one arm behind their backs. As we drove off, I noticed that as they brought their arm forward both were eating ice cream. Obviously, they were not genuine beggars and I would hate to think what would happen to them if the mafia caught them begging on one of the controlled traffic lights!

Karachi, passing Muslims on way to Synagogue

Shoe shine after being conned

With Gina at Taj Mahal

Nasurddeen and friends

With Rajan in Mumbai

With David Kelaty in London

Chapter 40

In 1986, Gina and I attended the Indian Rug Fair, which they had moved to the Taj Ganges Hotel, a much nicer venue and a larger event. We befriended a lovely couple there, Lakshmi and Ranu Raman, who owned a carpet business called Noble House. We instantly connected with them and had dinner on a couple of occasions. Ranu was into health food and mentioned that she had been told that Australia had very good muesli. Gina promised that she would send her some, which she duly did.

We visited Noble House, which was like a Havali or small palace as Lakshmi came from a very upper-class Indian family. His father was a good friend of Ravi Shankar, who was India's number one Sitar player. It is well known that the Beatles went to Varanasi to meet and play with Ravi Shankar. They stayed in Lakshmi's home in Varanasi when he was only a young teenager. He had no idea who those long-haired Englishmen were.

After attending the fair, we visited Bhadohi for a couple of days and then off we went on another adventure.

We went south to Cochin in the state of Kerala. Kerala is most interesting as it was the first Indian state to democratically vote in a Communist government in 1957 and since then has been voted in and out several times and was in power when we visited. It still has a Communist government today and has proven to be successful as Kerala is the most socially advanced state in India. It has universal Medicare and free education for all. 100% of both boys and girls go to elementary school. Kerala has the longest life expectancy and lowest infant mortality rate of any state in India and is the envy of all India.

At first, Gina felt very uncomfortable in Cochin. Being young and blonde didn't have the same movie star feeling that she encountered in Bhadohi. Here, the local men stared at her, in a sleazy way, making her feel cheap.

Cochin is a fascinating city as it had been a large trading port for many centuries with a picturesque waterfront dominated by large Chinese fishing nets and beautiful Colonial architecture. It also has a long and fascinating Jewish history. There is an area in the centre of Cochin that they call Jewtown. It is believed that the Jewish community settled there as far back as the tenth century, originating from Persian Jews. They are known as the Malabar Jews and are relatively light-skinned. The Paradisi Synagogue was built in 1568 and when we visited, we were shown through the synagogue by a local Jew who was the caretaker by the name of Jackie Cohen. In the evening, we walked the streets of Jewtown and were surprised to see many of the community outside playing cards whilst sitting at card tables. Most of the community have now emigrated to Israel and there are only about thirty or so still residing in Cochin.

There is a backwater trip that starts in Cochin and goes through to Alleppey further south. It is an unforgettable experience travelling through these backwaters. A water bus service travels the waterways, with regular stops, or you can travel the waters on traditional houseboats with modern amenities and a cook staying for several days.

We did a day trip on a water bus and as we were tourists, we were allowed to sit on the roof to get the best view of the picturesque calm tranquil waters and the surrounding beauty. The oldest houseboats were made from palm wood bamboo and were beautiful to watch as they meandered down the waterways. We saw lush paddy fields and plantations, masses of colourful floating waterlilies, an abundance of various birds, people using the waterways for transportation, children jumping into the rivers from the banks, fishing and daily chores. This is all part of local life and is their lifeline.

Further south was the city of Trivandrum. A small peaceful city that is near the bottom tip of India. It doesn't have the chaos, noise, pollution and dirt we saw in the other Indian cities and was a relaxing place to be. We had heard that there was a serene and unspoiled beach only seventeen kilometres away known as Kovalam so we took a taxi and headed there.

There was a steep hill as we approached Kovalam and as we were descending the hill, the taxi driver turned off the engine to save on petrol. So dangerous as the brakes didn't work effectively. I screamed at him to turn the engine back on. This is actually a common practice with taxi drivers in India.

What a stunning place Kovalam was. The beach wasn't crowded, had soft golden sands and the clearest of clear turquoise waters. Coconut palms lined the beach and lots of fishing boats with large nets were sitting on the calm water. There was only one hotel in the area called Rockholm that sat on the hill overlooking the beach but was quite expensive. Kovalam was gaining popularity with hippies and backpackers so most of the tourists stayed in small basic huts sitting amongst the coconut palms where local families rented out rooms. We found a lovely simple room owned by a young couple with a small baby, our host being a fisherman. There were a few beachfront cafes which were basic shacks serving local Keralan food, fresh fish and some international cuisine. These offered a relaxed, hippie-inspired vibe, so we felt at ease. We also ate a couple of meals with our hosts, fresh fish that he had caught, rice and fresh vegetables which we ate in the traditional way with our hands off a banana leaf. Our hosts didn't speak English but somehow, we communicated and enjoyed each other's company.

The sunsets were probably the most spectacular I have ever seen and we loved relaxing on the beach in the evening, smoking a chillum whilst watching the sunset.

We returned to Australia and were married on the 7th of April 1986.

Chapter 41

Our first son, Dan, was born in July 1987. After some time, as Gina was no longer working as a teacher, she felt that she would like to get back into some type of work.

My friend Rajan from Zeba had recently started a subsidiary business with his girlfriend at the time, Sonita. I had known Sonita previously as she worked as a designer at Shyam Ahuja and was very talented. Sonita and Rajan were producing a beautiful napery collection consisting of tableware, napkins, tablecloths, tea towels, etc and I thought it would be a good proposition to bring to Australia for Gina to get involved in. Gina liked the idea and thought that the samples I had selected from them were beautiful and we both believed there was an opening for Sonita's range in Australia.

Gina went straight out with the collection and sold it to David Jones, Myer, House, Minmax and lots of small homeware stores under the label Home Collection. Our first shipments were delivered to our home and the stock was spread down our hallway. In our second year, we took a stand at the gift fair and won the prize for the best new stand. The business was growing, so we fitted out our garage at home with shelving and this became our warehouse. The business grew further and Gina did a great job, however, as it was growing so fast, she required my assistance as she was now pregnant with our second child, our daughter, Sophie.

To continue Home Collection, we needed to open a proper warehouse and office and take the business to another level. It was becoming too big for Gina to handle on her own as she was also running our household and looking after young children. I was spending a lot of time, possibly too much, with Home Collection that it could be detrimental to the growth of Hali. As we could see a stronger and larger future in the Hali, we decided to close down Home Collection.

Chapter 42

The one store on High Street had been open for eight years and was doing extremely well but I had an ambition to expand and open more stores.

In my story so far, I have often referred in the first person to the achievements of the Persian Carpet Warehouse and Hali. That is because I realised that I had been the driving force in both businesses. I found all our suppliers and our agents in India, built up relationships in Europe, Turkey and Pakistan, found Shyam Ahuja and initiated enhancing and altering the design and colours of rugs to suit Australian tastes.

Many of my suppliers in India told me that when my partner came to purchase rugs, he would be very indecisive and confused as to what selection to make. I had a loving and warm relationship with my cousin and spoke to him about expanding Hali but he showed no interest as he was quite satisfied with our one store in High Street and had no further ambitions.

After many sleepless nights, I finally decided to break up the partnership, naturally causing a lot of friction. I suggested I would buy him out or was prepared to sell to him, deep down knowing that he would never do that but told him I was no longer prepared to continue in business together. We went through a terrible time, lots of arguing and as we couldn't come to a financial agreement, he took me to court. The court basically told us to sort out our own issues and come to a financial solution as it was not for a court to decide. We eventually agreed on a buyout figure and fortunately, Nick came to my aid by lending me the balance needed as I didn't have enough funds.

Chapter 43

Once it settled down and the business was mine, I thought about how and where to begin my expansion. I visited the rug department that David Jones ran within the furniture department in their Melbourne city store and felt that the stock was old fashioned, but being in David Jones had potential and I knew that I could improve it. I had front and confidence so I made an appointment to meet the David Jones Victorian manager and told her that they didn't have knowledge about rugs or what was in demand, that I did and if I took it over, it would greatly increase their takings. She listened! I arranged to pay them a percentage, took over the department and it became a store within a store, named Hali at David Jones. In no time, I improved the turnover greatly.

It didn't take long for management in Sydney to see the improvement and that I knew what I was doing so they invited me to Sydney for a meeting. They offered me the same deal to take over the rug department in their Market Street, Sydney store, which was a much larger department with approximately three times the turnover of Melbourne's. David Pickard moved to Sydney to run this establishment. It was successful and in a short space of time, we took over their Chatswood rug department in North Sydney, followed by Canberra and then in the new store that they opened in Rundle Mall, Adelaide. They were all branded as Hali in David Jones.

With the continual change of management within the furniture department, the stock mix kept changing. They were losing direction and with many new furniture stores opening offering a wider choice of furniture, the public stopped coming to David Jones for furniture.

Their furniture sales dropped dramatically, impacting our sales. I ran it successfully for twenty years but it was no longer viable for Hali to remain, so I moved out and established Hali free-standing stores nationally. However, the David Jones concession was a great asset in establishing the Hali Brand nationally as being genuine and honest.

My next venture was with Ken and Toni Robertson. They had a furniture store in Melbourne and they would purchase rugs from us for their clients. They went through some hard times and moved to the Gold Coast, opening a new furniture store, Robertsons on Bundall Road. They did extremely well and were still purchasing rugs from Hali for their clients. Within a couple of years, they moved to a much larger store on the same road and approached me to supply rugs for their in-store settings. I decided to fly up and meet them and see if this was worth doing as they weren't purchasing but wanted them on consignment. The store was beautiful. I was so impressed at the size of their store and the way in which they had fitted it out. There was quite a large area towards the back of the store that was still empty as they had plans to turn it into an in-store café. We went for lunch and jointly decided that a Hali store within Robertsons would be more profitable all round than a café. We shook hands and in no time, opened within Robertsons on a similar percentage deal that I had going in David Jones. Robertsons grew and became the number one furniture store on the Gold Coast. They would virtually sell rugs to their clients with all the furniture packages they were providing. Hali was becoming more established nationally and as there was very little competition on the Gold Coast for rugs, customers began coming into Robertsons purely to buy a rug, so we jointly employed a full-time salesperson to run it. It did extremely well.

Several years later, they opened a store in Brisbane. It had a perfect spot for Hali with its own separate entrance, so we continued the relationship successfully in Brisbane.

For over twenty-five years, I had a wonderful friendship and successful business relationship with Ken and Tonie. They retired and closed their business only a few years ago.

IAN SWART
RUG CONSULTANT

DAVID JONES (AUSTRALIA) PTY. LIMITED
A.C.N. 000 074 573
Melbourne Division
299 Bourke Street, Melbourne 3000
Telephone (03) 669 8200 Direct (03) 655 1642
Facsimile (03) 650 7937

To Whom It May Concern

Hali Retail Stores Pty. Limited ("Hali")
1114 High Street, Armadale, Vic, 3143

David Jones Limited has had a business relationship with Hali since 20 August 1992.

Hali has operated in our 299 Bourke Street, Melbourne store since August 1992 and currently has a Licence Agreement to sell handmade carpets within David Jones which has continued since that time and remains subject to 3 months' notice of termination by either party.

Hali has also operated in our Market Street, Sydney and Chatswood stores since 16 March 1998. The Licence Agreement for those stores currently extends to 15 March 2003 and then continues subject to 3 months' notice of termination by either party.

Hali took over the operations in our new Adelaide store at 100 Rundle Mall at the opening of that store on 1 September 2000. Whilst there is no formal document in place, the arrangements that apply are on similar terms and conditions as the existing Licence Agreements in the other locations.

Hali is an important ongoing partner of our department store business, they are our sole supplier of handmade carpets and the relationship is highly valued.

John A. Simmonds
Company Secretary

April 2001

David Jones Limited A.C.N. 000 074 573
A.B.N. 75 000 074 573
Market Street Sydney NSW 2000 Australia Telephone 02 9266 5544

HOME COLLECTION

Gina Swart
Mobile 018 554 915

759 Malvern Road
Toorak Victoria 3142
Tel (03) 827 9093
Fax (03) 826 0181

HOME COLLECTION

100% Cotton

Chapter 44

In the late 1980s, a hotel opened in Bhadohi. The Shiraz Hotel. It would be classified as a three-star hotel but it was new, and it meant that I didn't have to do the horrendous two-hour drive each day from Varanasi. They had one special room for overseas buyers, which was much larger and had air conditioning. Michael, my friend from Australia, joined me on this trip and when we arrived at the Shiraz, the buyer's room had been given to someone from Bombay. They immediately apologised so as he was out, they entered the room took all his stuff, placed them in a standard room and gave us the buyer's room. They left his used towel in the bathroom that had blood on it, making us both nearly puke. We slept on a king-size bed together. It was massive and classified as an Indian family bed. In the morning, I noticed a pair of shoes under the bed and asked Michael if they were his. No, they had left the Indian's shoes in the room!

I regularly stayed at the hotel and left Vegemite there for my morning toast, which they called Australian jam. About four years later, my brother-in-law, Rodney, joined me on one of my buying trips and I asked him how old he thought the Shiraz Hotel was. His reply was 'sixty years!' That's how it appeared after four years as it was now dirty. Everything was broken besides the fact that they were using the same towels as from the opening, which were now paper thin. I never stayed there again.

In the beginning, I stayed at the Varanasi Hotel but after a couple of years and from then on moved to the Clarks Hotel in Varanasi until the

Shiraz opened in Bhadohi. Once the Shiraz Hotel was no longer a choice, I went back to the Clarks.

Clarks was a very large hotel on massive grounds and a relic of the British days, which had a special appeal to me. It was owned and run by Upendra Gupta. He was an entertaining man in a very quirky way, with the limpest handshake I have ever encountered. I have spent lots of time with him at his hotel, as well as doing business together as he also had a warehouse with rugs which I purchased from. Upendra always talks business. One evening, we were having dinner together in his hotel restaurant when halfway through the meal, he collapsed, passed out and fell to the ground. His restaurant manager and staff all came running over. He came to but couldn't really speak so the restaurant manager and I carried him out to the car so they could drive him to the doctor. As we were placing him in the car, he looked at me and the first words he finally said were, 'What time are you coming to my warehouse tomorrow morning?'

Apparently, his collapse was due to a lack of salt. The next day he was fine and very happy to see me in his warehouse!

Upendra had a very interesting home. It was a large old home, traditional in style with lots of large old-style paintings, chandeliers and a dining room with a large mahogany table. He often invited me for dinner at his home. When entering, I would first sit in a lounge where I would be served spirits by one of the waiters from his hotel and offered various canapes. Much later, I would be called to the dining room for dinner where the table was set in silver service. A beautiful vegetarian Indian meal would be served. His wife would join us for dinner and they would put on air and graces but treated their servants poorly. I felt that I was back in the days of the British Raj.

From the grandeur of Upendra's home to the cultural dining customs in India, the contrasts between Indian and Australian hospitality traditions are night and day. Indians generally eat their dinner late at night. In Delhi, on one of my earlier trips with David, we were invited to a dinner party. We probably arrived at about eight p.m. We were offered drinks and lots of snacks kept coming. They were delicious and we kept eating them, assuming they were the meal. At 11.30 p.m., we were called into the dining room as dinner was being served!

We learned from then on to be very careful with the quantity of pre-dinner snacks and drinks to consume when attending dinner parties. The amount of dinner parties I have been to is countless.

Some of the larger wholesalers have guest houses in the villages for their buyers and I have sometimes stayed at Shyam Ahuja's, Rajan's, Hill and Co and Obeetee. These guest houses are quite charming and are often set on beautiful grounds with an abundance of servants looking after you; however, I didn't make a habit of this as it made me feel obligated to that supplier plus I enjoyed meeting friends in the evening, which you couldn't really invite to these guesthouses.

Chapter 45

There were times that I questioned the journey I was on. Life was so easy in Melbourne as I had all the mod cons and efficiency of the Western world.

The airports in India were small non-airconditioned tin sheds. Only one domestic airline called Indian Airlines graced these tired airports and they operated with tired old planes. They were stuffy, hot and so crowded, the stench of body odour all-consuming. You had to search to find a seat, often needing to sit in the corner on the filthy concrete floor. Invariably, you knew that the flight would be delayed. It was only a matter of how long, as delays were the norm. You could buy Limca, Thumbs Up and packets of biscuits or chips, not daring to eat any of the cooked food that was being prepared although I would sometimes eat a warm vegetable cutlet with lots of tomato sauce.

On one of my early flights to Varanasi from Delhi in an old plane, the seat belt came off its fitting. There I was, holding the seat belt in my hand for take-off and landing!

Another time, I was waiting at Varanasi Airport for my flight back to Delhi at four-thirty p.m. As usual, it was hot and stuffy in the old Varanasi airport, which had a few overhead fans that did little to reduce the heat. The departure time was written on a chalkboard. Four-thirty, then changed to five-thirty, then six-thirty, then seven-thirty then replaced by the word simple word 'late'! Never happened. At ten p.m., we were bused back to the hotel I started from and next morning taken back to the airport. The flight did take off but had a stop at an even smaller airport Khajuraho. We took off again after more passengers got off and on and *bang!* We heard a loud noise and were told that an eagle had flown into the engine, so we needed to land back at Khajuraho. After a few hours, the Indians staged an uprising. They had finally lost their patience and started screaming at the airport staff demanding a plane as they were not able to repair the engine. Several hours later, an empty plane was sent from Delhi to collect us. Thirty hours later, I arrived in Delhi, which should have been a one-hour flight.

On another flight, I was walking through the plane when I met a South African rug dealer that I knew. He asked where I was sitting, I looked back and could see that next to my aisle seat a leper was sitting. He was covered in a sheet, had a disfigured face and basically no fingers. I couldn't do it. I went to the hostess and explained nicely that I would need to disembark as I couldn't face sitting there. Fortunately, she found a seat for me closer to the front.

The more I thought about sitting in these sweltering airports or driving on the road to Bhadohi, I couldn't picture my life any other way as even on these uncomfortable days the sense of adventure in India was overwhelming and nothing was ever going to make me stop.

It wasn't until 1991 that India finally introduced the 'Open Sky Policy', allowing other airlines to operate domestically. The first to start operations was Jet Airways followed by several others. This changed travel in India dramatically. You now had a choice of airlines to choose from. They were new planes with improved service and more reliable departure times.

As the twenty-first century approached, new air-conditioned airports were built throughout India and in the cities I regularly visited. These are modern up-to-date airports in tune with the rest of the world. This made my travel throughout India much easier but I basically needed to wait twenty years before travelling in comfort in India.

Chapter 46

The late 1980s was a time of significant unrest in Kashmir. It was the only state of India that had a Muslim majority and they wanted independence from India. During this time, there was a rise in conflict between various groups and due to the escalating violence, it became increasingly dangerous for tourists to visit. For this reason, the Kashmir rug wholesalers moved their stock and set up warehouses in New Delhi so that they could continue business. In a way, it was a relief for me as it meant one less flight avoiding the delays and uncomfortable airports.

Mirza set up a warehouse in Delhi. It was a small building with several floors that went underground. I was in the lowest underground level that obviously had no fresh air or windows. I suddenly couldn't breathe and nearly passed out so Aezaz and Mirza had to carry me up the stairs to fresh air. It was a scary moment and I never went down there again. So for the next few visits, I would make Mirza's workers carry the rugs up to the ground floor. Not long after, Mirza moved to a warehouse attached to a new house that he built, which was a great relief. Every time he saw me, he would mention that time in his warehouse to the point of annoyance.

Aezaz introduced me to another silk wholesaler, Subash Mittal. Subash was one of the only wholesalers dealing in Kashmir silk rugs that wasn't from Kashmir. He had moved to Delhi from Bombay several years before and started the business from scratch. He had great taste and was honest; therefore, he and his stock really appealed to me and he became my principal supplier of silk carpets.

Subash was a wonderful man of a similar age to me and we built up a great friendship. We loved each other's company and every time I went to Delhi I would go to his office towards the end of the day, whether I was purchasing rugs from him or not. He would take a bottle of whiskey that was in a paper bag in the bottom drawer of his desk and we would have a few drinks together, then go for dinner, usually at the Bokhara, which is the most famous Indian restaurant in India and my favourite.

He and his wife visited Gina and me in Australia as did his son, Akash, and his wife, Arti, for his honeymoon. Sadly, Subash passed away several years ago from a terrible asthma attack.

He had suffered from asthma for a long time and about twenty-five years ago, he moved to the countryside in an area called Gurgaon, about twenty kilometres from the centre of Delhi, to have fresh air away from the heavy smog of Delhi, which is one of the most polluted cities in the world.

His son Akash took over the business and I have continued the relationship with him. We always go to the Bokhara together to keep up the tradition!

In 1990, a customer wanted a very large Kashmir silk carpet, so I needed to custom order it from Subash. It was to take one year to make. War had broken out, there was major armed combat taking place and the home in which the carpet was being knotted was attacked. I had to explain to my client that the rug was nearly completed but full of bullet holes of which I had a photograph as proof. They had to wait a further year for another to be made.

A very astute businessman that I know, or I thought he was until then, visited India and told me that he had met my supplier of Kashmir rugs. I asked where and he told me 'at the rug shop at the Moghul Sheraton Hotel in Delhi.' He actually believed that I bought my stock of Kashmir rugs from a hotel tourist shop.

Chapter 47

I enjoyed my moments in Delhi with Subhash and the times also with Nasrudeen and Aezaz. It is a great city and once you are used to the traffic chaos, it is fascinating and steeped in history.

It is a city of contrasts, every emotion and every experience that life has to offer is captured here in this sweaty and polluted bustling hub. In some parts, it seems that Delhi hasn't changed for centuries and in other parts, you feel you are in a modern metropolis. Old Delhi is a remnant of this past with historic sites like the Red Fort and Jama Masjid. Opposite the Red Fort is Chandi Chowk, the main road into the Old Delhi Markets, which dates back to the Moghul era. This road is chaotic with trucks, cars, cows, motorbikes, tuk-tuks and bicycle rickshaws. You can only enter the old Delhi market with its narrow lanes on a motorbike or bicycle rickshaw. A highlight is taking a rickshaw ride through the old market where masses of tangled electrical wires hang above you as you pass fabric stores with beautiful sari fabrics, stores with colourful beads and bracelets, toy stores with old-fashioned wooden and tin toys to the spice market where all the spices are presented in cone-shaped stacks and colour coordinated in a beautiful display and an amazing aroma.

Whenever I have taken someone with me to India, I have taken them on this rickshaw ride. It is very special and loved by everyone and I still get a buzz each time.

In contrast, New Delhi is a modern city with a blend of traditions and historic neighbourhoods alongside contemporary commercial and residential areas. Wide streets take you from the centre of New Delhi at

Connaught Circle to the beautiful Houses of Parliament, India Gate and the very modern diplomatic area and luxury homes. The feeling here is that you could be in a modern-day European city. They have built lots of flyovers and widened many streets in Delhi to cope with the enormous number of cars now on the road. A few years ago, they opened a very modern metro in Delhi, which has reduced the traffic and has made travelling around much easier.

Delhi was once called the city of billboards. Large billboards were everywhere but it was causing so many accidents as drivers were looking up at them so they became outlawed and subsequently all have been taken down.

Chapter 48

Domotex is the world's largest and leading trade fair for the rug and carpet industry. It's held annually in Hannover, Germany during January, usually a very cold and icy experience. European wholesalers, Turkish, Egyptian, Persian, Chinese, Pakistani and Indian manufacturers showcase their latest ranges of both handmade and machine-made rugs. It is a great opportunity for viewing the latest trends, networking and building business relationships. I visited the first Domotex fair held in Hannover in January 1989 and have been many times since. I have gotten to know so many people from everywhere in the world of rugs and learnt and exchanged many ideas as well as kept up with the latest trends rugs have to offer.

My first introduction to the large variety of Turkish carpets was on my first visit to Domotex. Until then, I was purchasing Turkish carpets from Kelaty whose variety and selection of Turkish rugs were quite generic.

One stand at the fair really impressed me with the range that they had on view. They invited me to visit their warehouse in Istanbul so I could see their full depth of stock. I took this offer up and after the fair flew to Istanbul to see their warehouse. They had an amazing collection and masses of stock. I worked my way through stack after stack, variety after variety and before I knew it, I had selected $100,000 worth of stock (remember, this was in 1989). They were the most trusting people I have ever met. They sent these rugs without any bank guarantee, totally on trust. The owner of the company's first name is Swat – we always laugh when meeting each other as my name is Swart!

Their head salesman was Mustafa and over time, we built a warm relationship and always looked forward to seeing each other. The food that I would eat for dinner and lunch with Mustafa, Swat sometimes joining us, was so different to what I experienced on my first trip to Istanbul in the seventies. We would sit at restaurants overlooking the Bosphorus, enjoying the tastiest fish ever, fresh from the strait, lamb that would melt in my mouth and the many varieties of meze being offered. Meze are small appetisers, a huge variety with a delicious range of Turkish flavours.

Before working in the rug industry, Mustafa worked as a tour guide. He told me that the guides would have a competition as to who could get the highest price for the lowest-costing rug. Invariably, it would be an Australian paying the most!

I came across another Turkish carpet manufacturer on my third visit to Domotex. Ipek, who produced rugs in the city of Izmir. The rugs of Izmir were different as they had more floral elements, soft tonings, a higher pile and very soft wool so I began to add Izmir to my Turkish trips.

Selecting rugs in Istanbul

Chapter 49

Once David Kelaty had taken over as the managing director of Kelaty, his younger brother Michael became the buyer. In the early 1990s, I introduced Michael to Nasrudeen in India and he became their agent for Varanasi. Michael and I we would often arrange to visit at the same time, spending a few days together selecting rugs. We had fun and if I was there without Michael, I would sometimes select rugs for Kelaty and arrange to have them sent to London.

Michael was keen to find an Arts and Crafts collection of rugs. I was not familiar with this movement.

The Arts and Crafts movement was a late nineteenth-century trend in decorative and fine arts. Its origin was in Britain and eventually flourished in Europe and the USA until the 1920s. It emphasized working with natural materials, simplicity and the beauty of handmade products. This movement had a lasting impact on design and architecture and is often referred to as the root of modern style. It was the incarnation of Art Nouveau in the early twentieth century.

William Morris was probably the most famous designer at the time and had designed a collection of handmade rugs. We found them. A company called Izhar were producing them for an American company, Natures Loom. I thought they were a fabulous look, something so different that I had never seen before, so I purchased them for Hali, promoted them and it became a successful range for Hali for many years to follow. Michael purchased them for England.

Chapter 50

With the success I was having with the Arts and Crafts carpets, I wanted to find an Art Nouveau range. Art Nouveau is more ornamental and intricate with more curves drawing inspiration from plants, flowers and animals. Unlike Arts and Crafts, I was aware of Art Nouveau.

Aezaz knew of a manufacturer that he had not done business with called Sabir who was producing a range for the USA. He took me to the most impressive showroom and warehouse. This showroom had a style that I hadn't encountered anywhere before. Most of the showrooms were quite basic, an overhead fan, no air conditioning and with very old uncomfortable dusty Indian furniture. Here, the furniture was modern, stylish and comfortable. There were rugs rolled up against the walls and even though I could only see the back of them, I could immediately tell that they were beautiful and couldn't wait to view his collection.

I excitedly sat and waited as the manager went to get Sabir. This handsome stylish man arrived and we were introduced. He looked at me, turned away and told me plain and simply that he wasn't interested in doing business with me. Australia was a small market and he wasn't interested as he specialised in the USA, which offered massive opportunities for him. He didn't want to entertain me in any way, didn't even offer me a cup of tea, which is customary in India. He had an allure of being aloof, smug, egotistical and basically threw me out.

Aezaz then informed me that his father-in-law was Badrudeen from Orient Arts and Crafts, who I mentioned earlier. We drove straight to see Badrudeen. I explained what had happened; he climbed in the car with us and we drove straight back to Sabir. In no fewer words, he told his son-in-law that I was a good honest Australian and that he was to supply me without question. Out of respect, he did what his father-in-law requested and business between us began and has continued until this day.

I introduced his Art Nouveau range to Australia. It is the only range of its kind in Australia and is still popular. Sabir also had a top-quality Persian design Tabriz collection better than I had seen anywhere so I bought them too and we still do.

It took a while but over time, he changed his attitude towards me. He began to respect my growth in Australia and the growth of the business we were doing together. I am now a very good client of his and he has become warm towards me.

Sabir is a master of colour. It is continually on his mind. One time, we were sitting, having a cup of tea together and he opened a packet of chocolate biscuits, held one in his hand and said, 'if I could choose a perfect chocolate brown colour, this is it', quickly calling his dye man in and handing it to him.

With his amazing colour sense and attention to detail, he has become so successful and wealthy that he built himself a huge house in Bhadohi. It is a mansion and a replica of the White House in Washington, boasting an elegant neoclassical façade supported by towering white columns. Behind the mansion is his warehouse and an office similar to what I imagine the president of the USA has. It is very decadent and certainly looks out of place on a dirt road in the village of Bhadohi.

His brother Javed, not a happy soul, turned to me once and said, 'We have all the money in the world and reside in a magnificent home, but when I walk out the front door I step into shit.'

I have always liked Art Deco and with the success of both the Arts and Crafts and Art Nouveau ranges, I thought an Art Deco collection would be the natural progression.

Art Deco carpets have clean lines and stylised motifs such as zig-zag lines, sunbursts and abstract geometric shapes. The colour palette is typically made up of deep blues, emerald greens, vibrant reds and gold.

Becky, who had recently started working with me, purchased Art Deco books and found some lovely photos of rugs. No one had been reproducing them, so I took a selection of the ones we liked best and gave them to a very competent manufacturer, Vimal Choudhary, in Jaipur to sample up. They were perfect so this became Hali's next exclusive look, which we still have success with. We remain the only Australian store with a collection of Art Deco carpets.

A couple of years later, French Aubusson and Savonnerie design rugs became popular overseas and Sabir naturally had the best selection so I purchased from him and launched this collection.

Another exclusive collection I introduced was a range of Ikat design carpets. These were based on the tribal designs usually seen on Sumba blankets just like the one I purchased in Jogjakarta in 1975 on my overland journey.

In the 17th Century Louis XIV presented Savonnerie carpets to foreign ambassadors.

Today, they are presented by Hali.

Chapter 51

Gina had not yet visited Turkey and didn't hesitate when I invited her to join me to visit Istanbul and Izmir in 1995.

We flew on Turkish Airlines. After a few hours of flying and hearing the Aussie voices in the row behind us, we began a conversation with them. They were both from Sydney and a similar age to me. I had a good feeling as there was something about them that looked interesting and I wanted to engage in conversation. Both had short, cropped beards and I got the vibe that they had travelled plenty probably during the seventies as I had. I think they got the same feeling about us. They were interested in engaging in conversation with us, asking what we did and why we were visiting Turkey. They told us that they wrote articles for travel magazines and were currently writing one about Turkey, having been invited by Turkish Airlines.

One of them was Glenn A. Baker, a legendary music journalist, author, radio and TV personality. He is world-renowned for his extensive knowledge of music, particularly rock and roll, and he is a respected authority on the subject in Australia. In the mid-1980s, he thrice won the BBC's Rock Brain of the Universe title. I came to know later that in 1995, Glenn won the Australian Society of Travel Writers Award.

The second man was Bob King, a respected music photographer. He is the longest-serving Australian rock photographer. Bob has photographed most of the world's top performers including the Beatles, Rolling Stones, David Bowie and Michael Jackson – the list goes on. His work has been featured in many exhibitions around the world.

They both loved travel, so they joined forces. Glenn wrote and Bob photographed as they travelled the globe writing for various travel magazines.

Coincidently, they were staying at the same hotel as us so we shared a cab from the airport and spent three days touring Istanbul together, having the absolute best and funniest moments. Our funniest moment was visiting the Istanbul Amusement Park, an old-fashioned fun park with rides, bumper cars and an old-fashioned Ferris wheel that we hopped on together that showed the sights of Istanbul from above.

We flew to Izmir so that I could visit Ipek and select carpets and guess what? Glenn and Bob were also heading there so we had more fun days with them seeing the sights of Izmir.

Izmir is a vibrant coastal city in Turkey. It has a beautiful waterfront promenade lined with restaurants offering superb views of the Aegean Sea. There is also a trendy neighbourhood called Alsancak lined with shops, cafés and bars. All in all, Izmir is a stunning city and we really enjoyed the relaxed atmosphere in comparison to Istanbul.

We drove together to Ephesus which is a UNESCO World Heritage Site an hour out of Izmir. It was an ancient Greek City dating back to the eighth century BC and would be the largest and most impressive archaeological site that I have ever visited. It is believed that the Virgin Mary lived there in her final years.

I selected a range of carpets from Ipek. They sold and I visited Izmir a couple more times but unfortunately, they went out of business and I couldn't find another supplier with the colouring and look that Ipek produced.

My regular trips to Turkey only lasted for about ten years after this trip and I loved my visits; however, over this timespan, handmade rugs from Turkey were disappearing mainly due to lack of labour and the labour cost. With each visit, I was finding less and less stock. Knotting carpets is extremely difficult work and the labourers can earn the same money working machines, producing clothing or leather, which is a much easier job so naturally, the labour source kept reducing as weavers left the industry. Turkey's production of handmade rugs has virtually disappeared. It now produces the most machine-made rugs in the world.

To be able to continue selling Turkish rugs to tourists, some Turkish manufacturers went to India with different designs of their rugs and had them copied. Nowadays, tourists are often being sold Indian copies of Turkish rugs when in Turkey and are being told that they are made in Turkey. The same with their silk rugs, the most famous being from Hereke, which are now copied to perfection in China and sold in Turkey.

On several occasions, acquaintances who have visited Istanbul have mentioned that they have met my Turkish rug supplier in a store at the Grand Bazaar. Surprisingly, such as my friend who had visited Delhi, they actually believed that I purchased my stock from a retail shop in the largest tourist bazaar in Istanbul!

These smart rug retailers have either heard of me through the industry or have searched the internet for rug companies in Australia. As soon as someone mentions they are from Australia, they tell them that they are the supplier to Mr Ian of Hali Carpets!

Endless times over the years, Australians have come into my store with a rug under their arm that they had purchased in Turkey from a very smooth salesman, which the Turkish are renowned for. They expected to sell the rug to me for a profit. Of course, they had paid an exorbitant price. I felt sorry explaining to them that they had paid a higher price than the retail price in Australia.

Chapter 52

In 1996, I travelled to America to the Atlanta Rug Show held in Atlanta, Georgia. Once again, I was the first Australian rug dealer ever to visit.

Whilst walking the hallways viewing lots of stands, I saw an Indian friend and supplier Naseem standing with another man and I went up to say hello. The other man was dressed immaculately and had a beautiful style with perfect teeth, a great crop of hair and a large Indian moustache. He wore several jewelled rings, an expensive watch and obviously looked very wealthy. He greeted me and knew my name. I couldn't place him. Later, upon walking into one of the stands, I saw a beautiful rug range called the Noble House Collection. I instantly realised that the man with Naseem was Lakshmi Raman from Noble House in Varanasi whom Gina and I had met several years earlier at the Varanasi Rug Fair.

I started walking the halls, searching for Lakshmi and when I did, I asked him if the Noble House Collection was his. It was. He had moved from Varanasi to the city of Jaipur, which was another rug-making region. He was manufacturing rugs there plus he was the buying agent for three wholesalers in America. Lakshmi then told me that his wife had never forgotten how Gina had sent her the muesli. He knew that I had an agent in the Varanasi area and offered to become my agent in Jaipur. I jumped at the offer. This man had great taste and top connections in Jaipur, and I was now part of his group.

Many stands impressed me and I could see now why the suppliers in India kept telling me that I had American taste. In contrast to the stands at the Indian fairs, these were modern, up-to-date and classy. Many were solid structures that were permanent fixtures and set up like stores even though they were only used twice a year. We were in the USA! Lakshmi was the agent for Bokara, Samad and Feizy, three of the largest American carpet wholesalers.

The Bokara stand is where I saw the Noble Collection range; at Samad, I saw beautiful rugs called the Golden Era Collection, which were made in Jaipur, and then I entered the much larger Feizy stand. John Feizy was standing at the entrance and as I introduced myself, he said, 'So you are the guy that is copying me in Australia.'

I was taken aback, amazed he had heard of me. Then he said it was fine for me to go in. He wasn't concerned as I was no threat operating in Australia, which was no opposition to him. His collection of rugs was superb. He was so nice and asked me to come back for lunch. At Domotex and Atlanta, Feizy sets up a dining area for his customers serving beautiful Persian food. So from then on, I was always welcomed and had lunch at Domotex and Atlanta in the Feizy stand.

At another stand, I also noticed rugs that had a different look and feel that I hadn't seen before. They were made in Nepal. I had seen rugs in Nepal in the 1970s but they were only of Tibetan designs due to their proximity to Tibet.

In the 1980s, an American, James Tufenkian, transformed the Nepalese rug industry by introducing modern and sophisticated designs altering the entire look of Nepalese rugs for the American market. He emphasized quality and craftsmanship and promoted sustainable practices elevating the reputation of Nepalese rugs. I thought the designs were beautiful and very interesting but I felt they were too expensive for the Australian market.

Chapter 53

I visited Jaipur and Lakshmi introduced me to a whole new world of rugs. There were lots of fabulous manufactures there and he took me to all of them. The rugs made in Jaipur were different. These rugs I was shown were traditional with a twist. What they had created in Jaipur were traditional rugs with the designs opened up, making the motifs much larger and allowing more space. This introduced a more contemporary look and colours had been altered to colours that were in vogue. These colours and designs were obviously targeting the US market and I loved them. I had never seen this look before and immediately started buying them. The Australian public loved them and they sold immediately. In fact, sales were so good that within a short time of receiving them, I flew straight back to Jaipur to buy more.

Being at the right place at the right time in Atlanta and meeting Lakshmi changed Hali, changed my life and lifted Hali to another level, introducing new beautiful rugs that had never been seen in Australia before.

Lakshmi was switched on and in tune with the latest trends. We got on so well. He had built a beautiful home for himself, Ranu and their son, Aditya. The home was white on a large piece of land with a sweeping driveway and several stories high, reminding me of a wedding cake.

He also had a superb collection of vintage cars and as I am a bit of a car lover, I admired them. He would take me to his mechanics and restorers to show me the ones that were still in progress. He obtained these cars by visiting Maharajas in various states who had old cars in need of restoration and would purchase from them.

I mentioned to Lakshmi the collection of Tufenkian rugs that I had seen in Atlanta but found too expensive so Lakshmi gave me the names of a couple of manufacturers in Bhadohi that Aezaz had never taken me to who were making the Tufenkian look at a much more affordable price. I arranged for Aezaz to take me there and suddenly I had another new modern collection to add to my ranges.

I called this the Himalayan Collection.

Chapter 54

Gina and I attended Lakshmi's son Aditya's wedding a lavish and unforgettable three-day event, which took place in both Jaipur and New Delhi.

An Indian Hindu wedding is an amazing celebration. They are quite diverse. Some are simple one-day events, others three days and some even go for five. This depends on both the strength of your religious belief and your wealth. Aditya's was a three-day event.

The first day was a pre-wedding ceremony held at the magnificent Rajputana Hotel in Jaipur, which was the city where Aditya lived as the pre-wedding ceremony is usually held at the city where the groom lives. It was an event where the groom and bride exchanged rings that they placed on their index fingers. Henna designs were then applied to the brides' hands and feet. This was accompanied by music, drinking and a spread of delicious food.

The second day, there was a function held at the home of Abhay, Lashmi's business partner. This began with an Indian wedding procession through the streets of Jaipur from Aditya's home to Abhay's. Traditionally, it is from the groom's home to the bride's but as the bride is from Delhi, it was held at Abhay's. A brass band led the procession dressed in what looked like Salvation Army uniforms. They made stops along the way where they formed a circle as close family members and some of the guests, including myself, danced in the middle. Next came a mobile stage with four musicians and singers. This was brightly lit by gas lamps. The groom followed on a decorated white horse, which wore gaily decorated embroidery, a mirrored saddlecloth and headgear.

Aditya wore a turban that had gold tinsel covering his face and a splendid white outfit with money given by guests as a gesture of good luck pinned to it. The bride was at the function awaiting the groom's arrival. Once again, there were drinks, dancing and lots more food.

On the third day, the wedding ceremony and reception were held at the Taj Palace Hotel in New Delhi. This was a beautiful traditional wedding ceremony conducted by a Hindu priest with the bride and groom exchanging flower garlands a symbol of acceptance and love. There were speeches, music, dancing, drinking and more food.

The three wholesalers from America that Lakshmi represented also attended: Gaby from Bokara Carpets, David Samad from Samad Bros and Amir Loloi, who was Feizy's cousin and vice president of his company. We got on so well and spent three days of continual laughter together.

We especially laughed when Gaby, David, Gina and I noticed we were always the first in line for the wedding buffets. We were all Jewish and it reminded us of the famous scene from the 1969 movie *Goodbye Columbus* where, at the Jewish wedding, everyone ran to be first at the buffet.

I also met Puneet Burman there who was a junior partner of Lakshmi and worked as his man for the Varanasi area. Puneet impressed me greatly.

Chapter 55

Business was growing with these new suppliers from Jaipur plus the ones that Lakshmi had referred me to in Varanasi, especially the Himalayan collection.

Lakshmi also suggested we travel to Agra from Jaipur, which was a four-hour drive, as he had a couple of manufacturers in Agra and the carpets made in that area had a different look to those from Jaipur or Varanasi. There was one supplier in particular who made a beautiful product he was sure I would want to buy.

This supplier made a collection that they had created by incorporating textile designs such as houndstooth, tweed, plaid, gingham check and herringbone. They blew me away. The wool used was strong and thick and the colour combinations were superb. I excitedly jumped at them and for many years, this collection, which I called Shalimar, became one of my best sellers. The owners were a couple called Gopal and Shephali, a friendly, well-read, intelligent and most enjoyable couple to work with. They looked similar as they both had the same crop of thick grey hair. They spoke with a very polished educated Indo-English accent and I spent many hours and dinners, even at Domotex, enjoying their company.

This opened up a new avenue for me and over time I discovered new suppliers in Agra adding another city for me to source rugs from.

Lakshmi also suggested more suppliers in the Varanasi area and I arranged for Aezaz to take me there. I could now see that there were many other manufacturers in the Varanasi villages with beautiful merchandise more suitable to my taste that I had not been exposed to so I began working with them.

As Lakshmi and I had become very close, I asked him if he would be prepared to work as a joint agent with Aezaz in the Varanasi region. He agreed. As Puneet was his man on the ground in Varanasi, I began driving around Varanasi and the villages with both Puneet and Aezaz in the car together. It was strange having two agents.

After some time, the three suppliers from America decided that they couldn't all work with Lakshmi as it was causing a conflict of interest. Bokara and Samad found other agents and Lakshmi retained the Feizy agency as this was his largest.

Soon after, Amir and his cousin, John Feizy – who he was working for – fell out and Amir started his own company. Lakshmi tried to be the agent for both, but Feizy wouldn't stand for this and broke away from Lakshmi. He convinced Puneet to leave Lakshmi and offered him the position of being his all-India agent exclusively. It was hard for Puneet to leave Lakshmi who he called Uncle (though he wasn't his uncle; it's a term many used in India to someone one respects) but it was an offer he couldn't refuse. Therefore, Puneet could no longer work with me.

I remained with Lakshmi and Aezaz but as Amir was taking a different direction looking more at a lower market to kick off his business, I became frustrated and found the suppliers I was now being taken to were not really suitable for Hali. I loved working with Lakshmi and thoroughly enjoyed his company but I realised it was time for me to move on.

With my front, I called John Feizy in America and said to him, 'John, you are a bastard. You have lumbered me with Lakshmi, taken on Puneet exclusively and I am now stuck with Lakshmi. I am not happy.'

He responded with, 'What do you want? Is it to work with Puneet?' I responded in the positive and he replied, 'Ok, I will contact Puneet and he can work with you.'

What a wonderful, generous reaction from someone I respected and who had become my friend.

One of the hardest decisions I have ever made was to leave Aezaz as my agent and appoint Puneet. Aezaz, Nasrudeen and their entire family were so good to me and we had become very close but for Hali to grow further, I knew leaving them was the correct step to take. It was also very uncomfortable and unnecessary for me to be travelling with two agents. I even got the occasional comment, 'Your business so big now you need two agents.' It was embarrassing! I knew that Puneet was the one that would help me grow my business further. It took me several months and many sleepless nights to build up the courage to make this move. I did.

Aezaz was understandably very upset. I couldn't do it face to face but only via a phone call. He didn't want to accept what had occurred and tried everything to win me back. However, I knew that this was the way for Hali to move forward. It was a difficult time, parting with Aezaz, and he took it quite badly. I was one of his largest clients and a close friend so obviously it hurt. Even now when I bump into him, it is quite uncomfortable.

Puneet was now my sole agent. He took me to new creative suppliers that he hadn't really wanted Aezaz to be exposed to. They were mainly dealing with the USA and had stunning trendy merchandise I had never seen before and obviously had not been seen in Australia. These suppliers were also the nicest people to deal with. In no time, Puneet was in tune with my taste and would always be on the lookout for new and exciting suppliers for me.

I kept several of the older suppliers that Aezaz had taken me to whose merchandise was still selling well or that I had found at the Indian rug fairs and dropped several others.

My relationship with Nasrudeen was different as I hadn't been working with him directly for many years. Nasrudeen's joint family business had separated years earlier and they each went their own way.

I would still always try and catch up with Nasrudeen on my regular visits as we still had a great friendship and loyalty to each other. He formed a new manufacturing company with his sons (he has nine children) but wasn't making merchandise that suited me so we hadn't conducted business together for years.

Approximately seven years ago, he contacted me to see if I could give him any work as he was struggling and needed help. Dhurries had been out of vogue for several years but I felt with new designs, it was time for a comeback. I selected a few designs and suggested he make samples. They were great. We ordered them and they have been very successful; in fact, we are still purchasing lots of dhurries from him. It got him back on his feet and he now supplies them to other buyers around the world.

I returned the favour I always felt I owed him.

Chapter 56

Puneet is Hindu, twenty years my junior and is a competent, wonderful agent as well as a trusted, true friend. He is still the agent for Hali and now deals with my son, Dan, who is twenty years his junior.

Besides our successful working relationship, we have had many wonderful evenings and lots of fun together. It is a joy to be in his company. He has taken me to lots of parties and introduced me to many of his friends. They are mainly Hindu so their wives accompany them and I find many of the wives a joy to converse with. This is something that I hadn't experienced in Varanasi before as Nasrudeen and his family are Muslim and mainly mix in a Muslim social group, which their wives don't tend to be a part of. I have enjoyed these parties with Puneet and his lovely wife Amrita immensely. He has entertained me for dinner at his home many times, which has also been joyous.

Puneet and Amrita are members of the Benares Club. It is a lovely club that is similar to the Bombay Gymkhana but smaller. It was established in 1962 and has many facilities such as swimming, billiards, cards, tennis, badminton, table tennis, basketball, cards, a children's playground, a function room and an indoor and outside restaurant. Families gather there in the evening to meet and enjoy the atmosphere and food. I have spent many an evening with Puneet, Amrita, their lovely daughters and some of their friends, enjoying the array of Indian snacks in the outdoor restaurant with the large outdoor screen showing Indian movies or, of course, cricket matches.

Puneet purchased an apartment in Gurgaon on the outskirts of Delhi, which is now a satellite city. Gurgaon has grown enormously from being a rural area when I first went there to visit Subash. It is now a large metropolis housing most of the large multinational, IT companies, call centres and the most expensive apartments. It has modern shopping malls and restaurants giving the feeling that you could be anywhere in the world. Puneet's apartment is lovely, and he invited me to stay with him so from then on, I stayed there many times when visiting Delhi.

The new Metro in Delhi went close to Puneet's apartment and we would catch the Metro to North Delhi where a driver would meet us to take us to Panipat for the day, which was the centre of the hand-tufted rug industry. By catching the metro, we would save a lot of time. It was eighty-five kilometres out of Delhi and a very non-descript boring place.

Hand-tufted rugs are a quicker form of making rugs, still made by hand but by holding a tufting gun and inserting the knots into a backing material. They are less expensive and became the entry-level rugs that Hali sold. As we sold lots of them, I needed to add Panipat to my regular India visits.

I would possibly know 200 people in India out of 1.4 billion so the likelihood of bumping into someone I know is miniscule. There, I was on the metro with Puneet, on our way to Panipat. I was standing near the doorway when Harsh, a younger man in his thirties who I was quite friendly with from Varanasi, stepped in at one of the stations right in front of me. Who would believe it! We engaged in conversation for some time until his stop.

Puneet made a comment to me after this meeting. He told me that what he admired about me was that I had a rapport with people and could communicate and befriend people of all ages. I have always treasured and thought a lot about that compliment.

With Lakshmi

Puneet and Aezaz

Chapter 57

I have taken all four of my children on trips to India at age eleven to experience the culture, beauty, history, poverty, food and smells of India and I believe they all have cherished these memories and this very special learning experience. They got to see both Old and New Delhi with its amazing contrasts from the markets of Old Delhi, the Red Fort to the modern cosmopolitan parts of New Delhi. The Taj Mahal in Agra, the beauty of the Pink City of Jaipur with its magnificent museum, the beautiful wind palace, the colourful markets and an elephant ride up to the Amber Palace. The grandeur and slums of Mumbai and of course, one of the oldest cities in the world – Varanasi with a boat trip down the Ganges at sunrise. Tuk-tuk rides racing around the towns and bicycle rickshaws through the winding lanes of the markets. Not to forget travelling the bumpy and fascinating road to see the rug-making villages, seeing where and how their father did his work. They would come back to school in Melbourne with small gifts for their class members and give a talk to the class about their experience.

As Becky is my oldest child, I obviously took her first. She experienced all the above and spent time in Bombay with Rajan's two sons, who were of similar age.

Child labour in rugs became topical in the late 1980s and rightly so. Children in the Indian villages worked on the looms as the poor village weavers could not afford to send their children to school so having their children stay home and work on the looms was a means to more income. The children's nimble small fingers could do finer knotting, which resulted in better pay that their parents were obviously keen on receiving. In 1986, the Child Labour Prohibition and Regulation Act was passed by Parliament, which prohibited children under the age of fifteen from working on looms. Even though this made things difficult for many of these poor weavers, they realised that for their children to have a better life with qualified jobs that education would provide, and free education was embraced.

The first organisation set up was called CLEWS (Child Welfare Eradication Society), which Nasrudeen was one of the founders of. The first couple of schools were in the surrounding areas of Bhadohi. I supported one by donating all the uniforms, books and a hot lunch for the 300 children each day. The cost of this was equivalent at that time to one term for one child at a private school in Melbourne. The school was named after Hali and myself, which was a feeling of pride and satisfaction.

When I took slides of the weaving of rugs for my course in 1979, many of them were photos of children weaving on the looms. Ignorantly, I never really thought about the child labour issue until it became a world topic. Now, thankfully, you do not see children working the looms during the day; however, it is not uncommon to see children working on the looms at home after school hours to help boost family income.

I took Dan, Sophie and Eli to visit the CLEWS school that I sponsored. Each time, we were treated like royalty upon arrival. The students and teachers would line up outside. Two students would place flowered lanyards over our heads as the children all clapped and cheered. The students would then run back to their classrooms to wait for us.

The classrooms were basic, furnished with old-fashioned desks with a lift-up lid, some only with floor cushions for the children to sit on. Chalk blackboards were at the front of the classroom. Once seeing these classrooms, my children certainly appreciated the comforts and amenities that their school in Australia provided them. We always arrived with a massive bag of lollies and I remember Dan, in particular, insisting on going from one class to another handing all 300 children a lolly. His back was very sore after!

We are now a sponsor for Care and Fair, a different organisation run out of Europe, which is the largest charitable organisation supporting no child labour and establishing schools to which we give a quarterly donation, a small percentage of all our total Indian purchases.

While I was working, Dan spent time playing cricket with the Ramesh family boys.

Sophie, my younger daughter, had a wonderful trip when she was eleven; however, I think she is scarred from the time I left her in the care of Aezaz's teenage daughters and nieces while I went off to work. They were somewhat amazed by this pretty, blonde, pale-skinned girl, fussing all over her, dressing her up in a sari and designing and painting her hands with henna.

Sophie often laughs and reminds me of this story about Aezaz. We drove from Delhi to Agra to visit the Taj Mahal and on the road back, we stopped at McDonalds, which had recently opened in India. We ordered Sophie a chicken Maharajah Mac. Aezaz ordered a fish burger but as it was Ramadan and the middle of the day, he couldn't eat so he kept it on his lap for about three hours until sunset, finally eating his fish burger on the outskirts of Delhi.

Eli spent time with the children of the Izhar family, playing video games on their TV. On the last two nights of our trip together, Eli and I stayed at the Taj Mahal Palace Hotel in Bombay, India's most famous and exclusive hotel. The Taj had mixed up our booking and as the hotel was full, they upgraded us to the Maharajah Suite, which had two bedrooms, two bathrooms, a dining area and a lounge plus three TVs. Eli looked around in amazement and commented on what a nice room it was as well as asking at the same time why we hadn't stayed in rooms like this every other night.

Dan had an extra special moment at the Taj Mahal in Agra. The tomb that the public gets to see at ground level is a symbolic monument and not the actual remains of Mumtaz Mahal, the wife of Emperor Shah Jahan. The actual remains are in an underground burial chamber beneath the main chamber. Once a year on the anniversary of the death of Mumtaz Mahal, the underground burial chamber is opened to the public and there both the actual tombs of Mumtaz Mahal and Shah Jahan are open for viewing. Dan and I were there on that one day of the year and were able to go down the steps and view them. It was a very special and memorable moment.

Eli also had a special moment at the Taj Mahal. He suddenly had a severe bout of diarrhoea; they were not the best toilets and I don't think it is something he really wants to be reminded of.

I took Becky on her second trip with me to India in January 1993. She was turning seventeen so Aezaz said he would arrange a birthday party. Can you imagine the joy of a seventeen-year-old girl having a party with about fifteen middle-aged Muslim men and no females! However they arranged a belly dancer for her, very weird! To top it off, the birthday cake arrived saying 'Happy Birthday Bucky'!

Dan and Sophie joined me on another trip to India and Kathmandu when Dan was twenty and Sophie eighteen. We stayed in Jaipur at a beautiful old Haveli, right in the centre of the Pink City. There were lots of monkeys in this area. I had a packet of cigarettes; for some reason, I smoked when in India but had given it up long before in Melbourne. The cigarettes were on the bed next to our three passports. I went outside to have a cigarette, leaving my door open. When I finished my cigarette and walked back to the room, a large monkey came out with my packet of cigarettes and sat on the doormat. It took each cigarette out of the packet, made a smoking gesture, and then broke each cigarette one by one. I called out, in fear, for it to go and a room boy heard me, came up with a big stick and chased it away. Luckily, he only took the cigarettes and not our passports! I went back into the room closed the door and tried to sleep. Every ten minutes or so, I would turn the light on in fear that maybe another monkey had also entered my room and was still there.

I thought it would be fun and interesting to go with Dan and Sophie to Kathmandu for a few days. Flying into Kathmandu is quite a memorable experience as you first see breathtaking views of the snow-capped mountains of the Himalayas then descend into a notoriously narrow valley with urban areas on each side, surrounded by lush green hills and terraced fields. Our arrival coincided with the beginning of the Hindu festival of Holi. Holi is a vibrant and colourful festival held at the beginning of Spring where people come together to celebrate the victory of good over evil and the blossoming of love. During Holi, people gather to throw coloured powders and water at each other, creating a kaleidoscope of colours. It is joyous and there is music and dancing.

We walked the streets had coloured powder and water bombs thrown at us from all directions. It was an incredible experience and we returned to our rooms looking like the colours of the rainbow and sopping wet.

I also thought it to be a great learning experience to take my sales staff to India, particularly to the rug-making villages, and see the actual process of rug making from dying the wool, hand spinning the wool, knotting the rugs, clipping them, the washing process, stretching and finally the drying process. This would give them more expertise and confidence when selling. So, I regularly took a member of staff with me. Also, I must admit, I enjoyed showing them around the country that I had fallen in love with!

This also established a bond between myself and my staff. I have always maintained a strong friendship with my staff but could still be authoritative when needed. Sometimes too authoritative as I knew how I wanted things to be done. Happy staff makes a strong business. Several of my staff members have stayed with me for up to forty years. I have always called the staff, and still do, 'my Hali family'.

One time, I took a staff member named Roger. He was a very English-looking man of my age with a finely cut moustache. We were on a flight together, sitting on either side of an aisle. I had a tomato juice. The hostess approached Roger and said, 'Would you like a fresh lime?'

Roger misinterpreted her Indian accent and thought she said, 'What is your first name?'

He replied very proudly, 'Roger.'

She looked at him in amazement, smirked and looked at me. I couldn't control myself but burst out laughing, knocking my tomato juice over my tray and on myself. She assumed he was this dotty middle-aged Englishman who was answering 'yes' as a pilot would, saying, 'Roger over and out.'

When Laurence, my Adelaide manager, came to Varanasi with Dan and me, he was in the breakfast room before us, diving into the food he had chosen from the bain-marie. This caused him to spend the next forty-eight hours in his hotel bed. I have learnt never to eat breakfast from a bain-marie in India as it is usually food that is left over from the night before but as he was in the breakfast room before us, I didn't have the opportunity to warn him.

I took Roberto, my Sydney manager, on another occasion and on his last evening in Delhi, just before his flight home, I took him to a restaurant called Punjabi by Nature. It has similar food to the Bokhara but much spicier. Apparently, he spent most of the flight home sitting in the small toilet cubicle.

On our first trip to London to visit Kelaty together, David Pickard – my longest-serving staff member – and I shared a small room at a hotel in Marble Arch as London accommodation is very expensive.

The week previously in Melbourne, Gina and I went to a friend's home for a dinner party. They had two Rottweilers; the larger one was called Arrow and I must admit, I feared Arrow. In London, I had a terrible nightmare of Arrow having me pinned to the ground and growling loudly just above my face. I woke up sweaty and in fright and then heard David's loud snore, which was the sound I heard Arrow make in my nightmare. David and I never shared a room again after that night!

Coincidently, this friend's sister also liked dogs and had a Doberman Pincer. David and I went to her home with rugs and were both scared.

I remember her saying as the dog's snout was near my crotch, 'Don't worry, the dog is fine as long as you don't look him in the eye.'

We had to go back a few days later with different rugs and when we rang the doorbell, we insisted that she lock the dog up or we wouldn't enter her home.

Chapter 58

In the late 90s, David Kelaty invited his buyers from all around the world to a three-day golfing event at one of England's most exclusive golf resorts with all expenses paid except airfares. I attended three of these events. My golf was non-existent, so I quickly had a few lessons and tried my best which wasn't great but nevertheless, it was something I wasn't going to miss out on.

The first one was held at Hanbury Manor, which has an eighteen-hole championship golf course. David Pickard joined me. The hotel was a magnificent building with a palatial appearance and had elegant accommodations that were historic, blended with modern facilities. It had several restaurants, a spa and wellness centre, tennis courts, walking and jogging trails.

It was a wonderful opportunity to meet rug dealers from around the world. They came from within England, different parts of Europe, South America, South Africa and the USA. I gained a lot of rug knowledge from meeting these dealers and discussing various aspects of the rug industry. We had the best time mixing with them, establishing new contacts, having wonderful breakfasts, lunch and dinners, drinks and playing terrible golf.

The second event twelve months later was held at Mannings Heath, which had facilities and accommodations similar to Hanbury Manor but offered two eighteen-hole championship golf courses. Somehow with my terrible golf, I managed to win the prize for nearest the pin.

Becky had been living and working in London at that time so she joined me. As I hadn't seen her for months, I forgo some of the games and we had a beautiful time together.

Twelve months later, I attended again and it was back at Hanbury Manor. Gina joined me this time but didn't play golf. She befriended an elderly Jewish New Yorker named Gerry Weinrib who also didn't play so they spent time together during the day when the rest of us were out playing. He adored Gina.

Gerry owned the ABC store in New York, which was the largest retail carpet store in the world. In New York a year later, we went to visit him in his store and as we entered the office reception, he screamed out to his security, 'Get this riff-raff out of here,' obviously in jest.

He was so happy to see us. Well, Gina, that is! He took us for a tour around his massive store, spanning eight floors. Three floors were dedicated to rugs the others with homewares and furniture. We had a beautiful lunch with him at his in-house restaurant and bought a lovely Art Nouveau lamp, which we carried home and still have.

David and I at Hanbury Manor

Chapter 59

In 2001, the CEPC (Carpet Export Promotion Council) started the All-India Carpet Fair, which they held in New Delhi in March at an exhibition centre called Pragati Maidan. This fair showcased rugs from all parts of India including the Varanasi region, Agra, Jaipur, Kashmir plus jute rugs produced in Southern India. They offered an incentive for buyers from around the world to attend.

Australian buyers were offered two nights' accommodation at a five-star hotel including breakfast plus transport back and forth from the fair. We were also given US$700 – first in the form of travellers' cheques and later in cash once we had shown proof that we had attended two full days at the fair and produced a copy of our return airline ticket.

With this incentive, I started seeing several other Australian buyers coming to India.

It has been an extremely helpful fair for me and I have certainly found some excellent products and suppliers there. I would usually spend the first day walking on my own and on the second day, Puneet would join me so I could take him to stands, which I thought were worthy to visit with the possibility of starting a future business.

Being the Australian pioneer in the industry, everyone knew me and I must admit it drove me crazy at times as I would walk down the various hallways and people would call out, 'Mr Ian' or 'Mr Hali, please come visit my stand and see my carpets.' Sometimes, they would even come out and try and grab me.

At the same time, it was also enjoyable for me to catch up with the many people I knew, some of whom I possibly hadn't seen for ages as I didn't necessarily do business with them anymore.

I never got my clothing right at this fair as they couldn't seem to get the air conditioning working efficiently. One aisle was freezing, the next cool and at a perfect temperature, the next one boiling hot.

Chapter 60

Some of my close friends had never been to India, but they had heard me talk so often about how I found it to be the most fascinating country. They asked if I would take them on a tour so in March 2005, Gina and I took six couples on a trip that they called 'Ian's Magical Mystery Tour of India.' This was written on a yellow sash with purple writing, which we all wore laughingly on our flight over.

I wanted to take them on a most memorable and wonderful tour, so I planned something very special.

We started in Mumbai and stayed at the Taj Mahal Palace Hotel. We had a beautiful cocktail party at my friend Rajan's apartment, which has a 360° view over the city. From there, we took a horse and buggy ride at night through the streets of Mumbai. The next day, we toured Mumbai.

We flew to Jaipur where we stayed at the Rambagh Palace, rode around on bicycle rickshaws and auto rickshaws. We took an elephant ride up to the Amber Fort, the markets, City Palace and the observatory, then drove into the desert to Samode where we stayed in a permanent tent-style hotel and took a camel safari.

Next was Delhi and we stayed at the Imperial Hotel. Since the times I had stayed there many years before, the Imperial had undergone a massive renovation. In fact, it was the nicest renovation of a hotel I have ever seen. The Imperial Hotel is now amongst the most beautiful luxury hotels in the world, still retaining the Colonial feel that I loved.

We toured Old and New Delhi in a minibus with a guide that I arranged and as we were approaching the Red Fort, we couldn't control ourselves from laughter when our guide called out, 'There it is over there, see where I am fingering.'

I had also arranged a dinner at the Bokhara. We all placed on the traditional bib they give you and the meal lived up to my expectations – they all couldn't believe how delicious it was.

On arrival at Varanasi Airport, we were greeted by some of my Indian friends holding up a banner that stated, 'Welcome Ian Swart and Friends.' It was a lovely gesture.

I wanted them to have a bit of the Indian hotel experience that I had undergone for many years, so I took them to the Clarks Hotel to stay. They were quite shocked as this was probably the only place where they were not so happy but to their credit, they laughed it off.

Upendra owns a small Havali overlooking the Ganges River near the ghats and arranged a magnificent vegetarian dinner for us there. It was nice that John Feizy was in town so he joined us with Puneet and Amrita for this very special dinner.

I arranged an early morning visit to the ghats and a boat ride along the Ganges, which naturally blew them away. After breakfast, we took a minibus on the incredible road to Bhadohi where they saw all the processes of making rugs and got to see how I work in this remote village. An afternoon tea for all of us and some suppliers was held at Ramesh. They couldn't quite believe that this was where I had visited so many times and conducted the bulk of my business.

After visiting Bhadohi, we got back onto the minibus and they took a video. Tommy, one of my friends, said the following, 'If you believe Hali rugs are expensive, you are wrong. They are cheap as I have now seen how many processes go in to make one carpet and to what lengths and difficulty Ian travels to purchase them. He should put his prices up!'

Back to Delhi and they all went off for a day trip to the Taj Mahal. Next morning, I said goodbye to them, including Gina, as they all headed to the airport. I stayed back in India, heading off to the villages to work for a few days.

They have all told me that it was the most fascinating trip that they have ever been on.

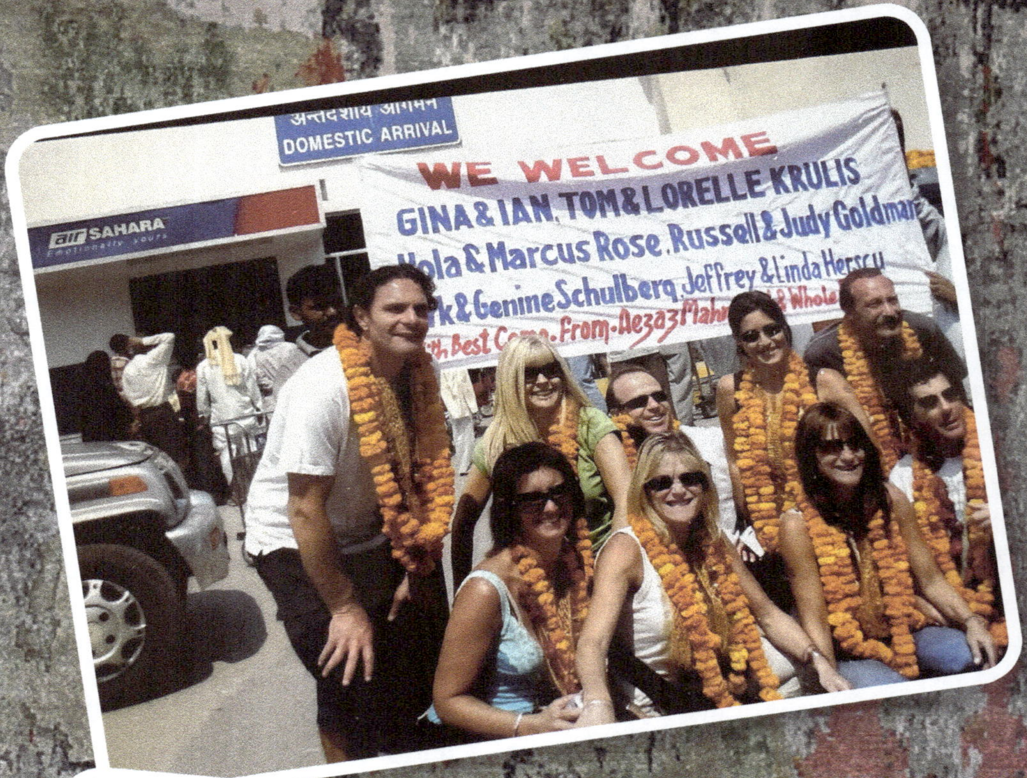
DOMESTIC ARRIVAL
air SAHARA
WE WELCOME
GINA & IAN, TOM & LORELLE KRULIS

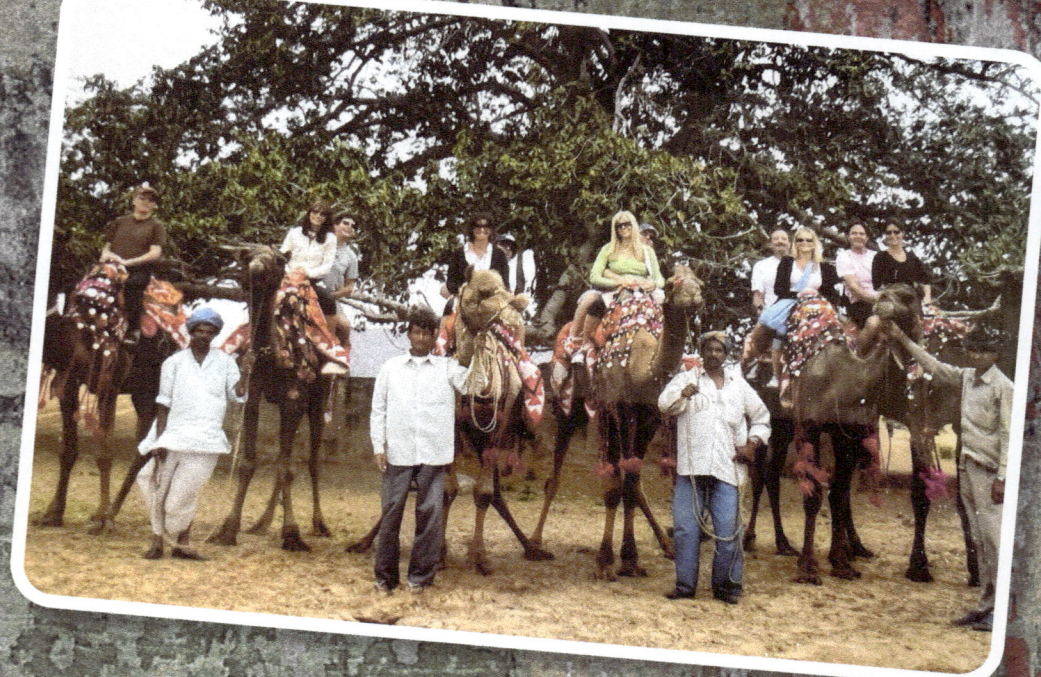

Chapter 61

In November 2006, my son Dan was in Goa. He was on the way home from Europe where he had been travelling with his friends for months on their gap year. As I was in India on a buying trip and as I hadn't seen him for over six months, I flew to Goa.

They were staying in Vagator, a small coastal village north of Anjuna, the place where I had stayed twenty-seven years before. The only taxis available at the airport were small Suzuki vans with a seat placed in the rear. It is a fifty-kilometre ride on a bumpy road that travels partly along the picturesque coastline and inland through small towns with bustling markets on the main road. As you drive back towards the coast on a winding road with hilly terrain, you approach the small town of Vagator. The trip took about an hour and a half in this hot little van but I was so excited to see and be with my son.

He was waiting at the bus stop where we agreed to meet and we enjoyed a big hug! He had obviously been travelling on a low budget and told me there were seven of them sharing a house, sleeping on mattresses on the floor with a basic kitchen and one bathroom. They were paying about two dollars a night each. I knew all seven as Dan had been friends with them most of his life and looked forward to seeing them all.

Then he said to me that he had booked me the best hotel in Vagator, and nervously added, 'I hope you don't mind but it's thirty dollars a night.'

Cute how your standards change when on the road on a budget. Most hotels at that time were costing me $150 a night. I hopped onto the back of the motorbike he had rented and rode to my hotel.

My hotel was small and basic with a double bed, no furniture, a concrete floor and an ensuite bathroom. However, outside of my room was a bench to sit on and a swimming pool in the centre courtyard surrounded by about ten rooms.

We went for a stroll down towards the beach and there was basically a narrow street dotted with small shops, guesthouses and a few small restaurants catering to the tourists.

Vagator was a hidden gem with its laid-back picturesque, untouched and undeveloped beach compared to some of the more developed beaches in the area. Most of the travellers were hippies, backpackers and alternative travellers with a focus on music, art and alternative lifestyles.

I visited Dan's friends at the house, receiving joyous hugs from all of them. Then I was offered a joint and felt like I was reliving my youth!

I took them all out for dinner a couple of times and had lots of fun with this great bunch of kids that I knew so well.

I asked Dan to take me to Anjuna Beach on the motorbike the next day to see if it was still the same. There was still a hippie culture; it still had the flea market and the stage for bands on the beach. The main difference I noticed were many more small cafes along the beach.

I stayed for three days and when alone at the hotel, I would roll myself a joint, relax on my outdoor bench, jump into the pool to cool off and reminisce about my time in Goa twenty-seven years before, the time when Becky took her first steps.

Chapter 62

I enjoyed the many years of selling rugs while I was on the sales floor. I have always liked design and I have been fortunate to visit some of the most beautiful homes throughout Australia. I would get a feeling of satisfaction and pleasure that was not purely financial when my suggestions worked in adding a new dimension to a client's room.

There are two phrases that customers say with monotony to a rug salesperson. I have heard these said thousands of times and when I walk into the stores these days, I still hear them. The first is whilst flipping the stacks of large rugs: 'You don't need to go to the gym while working here.' The second is when telling the price: 'When I win Tattslotto, I'll be back.'

My favourite rug joke is this one: an elderly lady came into a rug store and the salesman showed her through the large stacks. As she bent down to feel the texture, she farted and, embarrassed, said sorry. The salesman told her not to worry and continued flipping. The same thing repeated, the same apology and the same don't worry. A third time, it occurred again. The salesman abruptly said, 'Don't worry, madam, but when I tell you the price you will shit yourself.'

The worst comment we hear from clients is when they walk in and ask for a 'mat'. You know from that comment that they have no understanding and if you do end up selling to them, it will certainly not be a large sale.

Selling hasn't always been smooth sailing though.

One Sunday morning at about eleven a.m., I backed into a driveway in Toorak at the home of people I knew well – the Wittners – and carried a rug inside. As I left and drove forward, I felt a bump then another bump. I saw their poodle fly up in the air behind my car. It had laid down in front of my wheel after I had backed in. It was on the road in pain. I went to console it and it gave me the kiss of death, between my thumb and forefinger. I pried open its mouth to release my hand and it died. Very sad but as I knew the family, Mrs Wittner stopped my bleeding with a band-aid, antiseptic and a scotch to settle my nerves while her husband and son gathered up their dead dog. Mr Wittner indicated that I probably did the family a favour as the dog was old and deaf, so I left in the Hali way: with the money for the rug in my pocket. The dog's name was Peanuts so I went home and told Gina I had sadly crushed peanuts!

Another time I went to a large Edwardian Mansion home in St Kilda with two rugs to select from for their entrance hall. They selected one and as I was about to leave, I threw the other over my shoulder and *crash!* I totally smashed their overhead antique chandelier. I replaced it and can honestly say that this is the only time that I have lost a serious amount of money when selling a rug!

In a different, more modest home, I turned whilst holding a rug and smashed a vase that sat on a mantlepiece. I don't think it was a very expensive one as they didn't ask for any money and paid me in full for the rug; nevertheless, it was a most embarrassing experience.

One evening after work, I took a rug to sell at a house in Melbourne. It was in between my marriages so I was not in any rush to get home. After making the sale, the homeowner offered me a whiskey, which I naturally accepted. We were enjoying each other's company and I was offered another and another and another. I got so drunk that I could hardly stand up let alone drive home so the lady of the house got me a blanket and I went to sleep on their couch. I woke up at about six a.m., embarrassed. I sneaked quietly out of their house and drove home. Luckily, they had paid for the rug so I didn't have to go back and confront them.

David's experience with a rug sale was quite laughable, although not for him. He went to a lovely, renovated home in Malvern, which belonged to a well-known TV personality. They had brand new white carpet down the hallway and he had to carry the rug down the hallway to the family room at the back of the house. Would you believe he had stepped in dog poo before entering the home? He spread it all along the hallway on the white carpet. He spent the next hour on his knees with a bucket, rag, soap and water cleaning the carpet. David, being a true Hali salesman, left there with the money for the rug in his pocket.

Chapter 63

When I first started visiting India, the population was approximately 500 million. It has increased by about twenty million per year so now after forty-five years of regular visiting, it has blown out to about 1.4 billion! So, I have certainly experienced a massive change.

As you can well imagine, the traffic in India is chaotic. Cars weave in and out and it amazes me that I haven't seen loads of accidents. I have, fortunately, only been involved in two minor ones. Once at night driving in Delhi with Nasrudeen, his driver hit a pedestrian who stepped in front of the car. He flew up and landed on the ground. He lay there and we drove on. I asked why we were not stopping to assist and they told me that no matter whose fault it was we would be put in jail until the situation was resolved so we drove away.

Another time I was driving with Aezaz, in a country area on a large road when an Indian on a motorbike swerved right in front of us. Our driver couldn't stop, and it certainly wasn't his fault. The guy flew up in the air landed on the bonnet and fell on the ground, his motorbike mangled. I thought he was dead. This time, we stopped. He got up, fortunately, and went to the driver's side, who put his window down. The man started hitting our driver like crazy and tried to pull our small-framed driver out through the window. I lost my cool, jumped out of the car, grabbed the man and pushed him away. He fell to the ground. It was a very stupid thing to do as, by now, villagers had all arrived to see what had happened. Luckily, no one took revenge on me. To settle things, Aezaz handed the man some money to repair his bike and we went on our way.

Countless times I have been caught in traffic jams that can seem to last forever. The worst one I experienced was in the car with Dan when he was young. We were with Lakshmi, travelling from Jaipur to Agra, a four-hour drive on a two-lane road. Trucks and cars overtake each other and when we were possibly half an hour out of Agra, we were gridlocked. So many trucks had overtaken each other that we ended up with lots of trucks and cars each facing each other with nowhere to go. Cars and trucks kept coming and the lines became longer and longer. Police arrived and seemed at a loss as to how to sort it. The cars and trucks that were on the wrong side of the road began to reverse. As there were such long lines on both sides, this seemed to take forever. There were a couple of small side roads so they were forced to move into them to help. I think it took about another two hours before the problem was sorted.

I lost my licence once for speeding. When I mentioned this in India, they all answered with the same phrase: 'How is this possible? Why did you not pay the policeman?'

Bribery was always common in India. Peter, Aezaz's son, was thirteen years old when he decided to get a driver's licence. He drew a moustache on a photo of himself and arranged for an adult to take it to the police station, bribe the policeman and there it was, he had a driver's licence!

Visiting the same airports and hotels so often, the doormen and porters all know me. The managers and reception staff changed more often, but the doormen and porters remained.

At Varanasi Airport, the same porter has found me for forty years and has always carried my luggage. He was eighteen at the time and they only just retired him at age fifty-eight. He is a lovely man and I always tipped him well. A few years ago, I decided I would give him an amount he had never dreamed anyone would so I gave him a few hundred dollars, which was probably about six month's pay. He was in total shock and naturally so appreciative. He couldn't believe his luck. I have repeated this with him. During Covid when he was out of work, I sent him some money. He has my mobile number and recently contacted me to invite me to his daughter's wedding. I didn't go but sent a sum of money as a wedding gift.

When I arrive at the Taj Hotel in Varanasi or the Rajputana in Jaipur, the porters always greet me and ask me how my children are as they have met them all and have known me for many years. I have also given them a few hundred dollars in recent years as it means so much for them and fortunately, I can afford to give.

It has always amazed me, and still does, how the Indians seem to have respect for a Westerner after the treatment that they received from the British during their domination. I have often been asked if I am a Britisher and am always referred to by employees as Sahib and Gina as Memsaab in a respectful manner.

Chapter 64

Doing business in India today is very different to when I started. In the beginning, we did our correspondence via a telex machine, which sometimes took a few days for a response.

Suppliers would post an envelope from India with photos of their newest rugs, but they were never a true indication of what the product looked like and were of little use to me. We didn't have mobile phones. To make a call to Australia from India, you needed to book through the operator. The operator would request that you 'furnish' the number, a very old English phrase meaning to supply one with what is needed – a remnant of the British influence. I would sometimes wait two hours for the call and when it finally came through, I would get to say 'hello' and a couple of other words and *bang!* I was disconnected. To try and call a supplier in India was just as hopeless.

Fax machines followed, which gave you an immediate answer and now, thankfully, emails, which are even more immediate as you can view these on your mobile phone or computer wherever you are. Photos on mobile phones or attached to emails add another dimension as they give a true indication of what the rugs look like.

It is still tough and hard work travelling through India for business but now with beautiful hotels, refrigeration, food not being an issue, new planes, a competitive network of airlines with modern airports and modern airconditioned cars, bottled water plus the luxury of having your mobile phone operating for you wherever you are, it has made it a lot more palatable but I guess it has taken some of the adventure away that I experienced for many years.

To arrange a visa for India now is also simple compared to the early days. For many years, I would need to go to the Indian visa office in Carlton, take a number and wait in line, which seemed like forever as the office was always packed, before handing in the forms and passport, which were sent off to the Indian embassy in Canberra for approval. Two weeks later, I would need to go back to the Carlton office once again, wait in line forever and be handed back my passport with a six-month visa stamp in it. On arrival in India, I would stand in another long line to be eventually questioned by a customs officer before he stamped my passport and allowed me entry.

Now, you can arrange a five-year e-visa by email and on arrival in India, scan it through the machine and walk straight through to the baggage collection.

Chapter 65

In May 2024, I completed a trip to India with Dan and his father-in-law, Danny. I had only travelled to India once in the past four years due to Covid and my retirement. As this was Danny's first trip to India, I suggested I come along and show him the sights and of course, this was a good excuse for me to visit that special place.

Showing Danny the sights of Delhi, Varanasi, Agra, Jaipur and Mumbai from the eyes of a tour guide, I noticed many changes in India.

The most obvious change I noticed was the cleanliness of the roads. Prime Minister Modi introduced the Clean India Mission in 2014. The effectiveness of this policy is now evident even on the road to Bhadohi.

Modi promoted the cleaning of all roads by employing three million government workers and students from all parts of India to sweep the roads twice daily in over 4,000 cities, towns and rural areas. As an Indian man said to me, 'Our roads in India have now become spick and span.'

This has amounted in awareness by the public, communities and local government all actively and proudly participating in cleanliness drives. You continually see locals sweeping outside their homes and businesses so now the streets are clean and devoid of rubbish, which had always been strewn everywhere.

Cows, which are sacred animals in the Hindu religion, have always roamed the streets in the major cities, towns and rural villages. In the cities, this caused major traffic issues as cows would often lie down in the middle of the roads, causing havoc and traffic jams. Plus, of course, defecating wherever they pleased. The government has implemented initiatives with the help of municipal authorities to carefully remove stray cows to cattle shelters and rural areas to ease the traffic conditions and maintain the cleanliness of the roads. Major cities are now devoid of stray cows roaming the streets.

Another important initiative Modi introduced was the construction of toilets throughout urban and rural India to eliminate open defecation. Millions of toilets have been built.

In the India I have always known; the cities were choked with older cars emitting black exhaust pollution. To address this issue, Modi introduced the 'Vehicle Scrappage Policy 2021', which aimed to the scrapping and replacement of old and polluting vehicles with newer and more environmentally friendly models to promote a cleaner and more sustainable automotive ecosystem.

Under this system, commercial vehicles over fifteen years old must pass a fitness certificate whereby vehicles undergo periodic fitness and emission tests or be scrapped. Private vehicles that are twenty years old are not permitted to enter the cities. There are vehicle fitness tests in place and incentives for purchasing new cars and electric vehicles.

I certainly noticed the air to be cleaner but Danny couldn't understand that the air was much improved.

Modi also introduced a focus on waste management with the promotion of clean and green practices such as composting and recycling.

Our first stop on this trip was Delhi. With all the new roads, flyovers, the metro system, no cows roaming the streets and the regular sweeping of the roads, I noticed a huge improvement in the traffic flow throughout this enormous heavily populated city.

We visited Chandi Chowk in Old Delhi, which I described in chapter 47 as being chaotic with trucks, cars, tuk-tuks, cows, etc causing havoc along the road. Now they have gates at the entrance to the road and have turned Chandi Chowk into a mall, allowing only bicycle rickshaws and pedestrians to enter. They have built a divider on the road, making it easy to walk or sit in a rickshaw as you enter the market.

Varanasi is situated between Kolkata and Delhi. The main road, MG Road (Mahatma Gandhi Road), that connects the two major cities runs through Varanasi. This always caused havoc and traffic congestion as many trucks drive between the two major cities. They recently opened a bypass road so the trucks do not enter Varanasi, relieving this congestion.

The MG Road has been widened and turned into a major highway with a division down the middle, with intermittent openings. In typical Indian fashion, though, you encounter drivers coming towards you on the wrong side of the road as they don't want to waste time looking for openings.

Agra is a city that I have always disliked as I found it dirty, cluttered and, except for the Taj Mahal, uninteresting. This time driving through the city, I was quite impressed as it is now less congested with the roads being clean and no cows causing traffic chaos. Previously, you could drive close to the Taj Mahal and walk to it. Now, they have stopped traffic driving within two kilometres. There is a large parking area and from here, you catch a small electric shuttle bus to the monument, preserving it from pollution.

In Jaipur, I have often taken the very touristy elephant ride up to the Amer Fort. At the base of the fort, there was always a huge line-up of colourful elephants, with painted trunks and a colourful canopy to sit on. This time we arrived and there were none. Due to protests for world animal protection, most of the elephants have been retired. There are only a few elephants still taking tourists and these animals live at the base (previously, many lived several kilometres away and had to take a long walk home). They are looked after and fed well. During the hot summer months, they are only permitted to carry tourists from eight a.m. until ten-thirty, avoiding the heat.

I also noticed that there were no camels on the roads in Jaipur, something which I was always aware of. Once again, concerns for animal rights have stopped these animals being used for commercial purposes on city streets.

The market in the centre of Jaipur was always very alive with local people in traditional clothing. Many of the women still wear the beautiful colourful saris but the men, who used to be in abundance wearing traditional colourful turbans, have all but disappeared. Westernisation and globalisation have influenced men's attire and there has been a shift to Western-style clothing. Women tend to prefer wearing traditional saris as part of cultural tradition and for comfort as the flowing fabric allows for air circulation, keeping them cooler, especially in the hotter and humid areas.

I hadn't been to Mumbai for several years. Driving from the airport to Colaba would always take approximately an hour and a half as you wove your way through many narrow streets choked with traffic. Now, there is a six-lane divided trans harbour link that has been built over the bay, which is twenty-one kilometres long and takes you into Mumbai in about twenty minutes. They have just opened a tunnel that now joins the harbour link road to Marine Drive in Worli, which is only a ten-minute drive to Colaba.

Marine Drive, which is a lovely coastal road in Mumbai, now has a wonderful walking promenade along the beach, a very popular spot for walking as the sun sets over the water. The buildings on the opposite side are beautiful examples of Art Deco, still quite dilapidated but now many are being renovated. All these buildings have recently been classified as a UNESCO World Heritage Site. Mumbai is home to the world's largest collection of Art Deco buildings after Miami. One day, this promenade will be one of the finest examples of Art Deco in the world.

The main railway station in Mumbai is a stunning example of Victorian Gothic Revival architecture. I had never walked from Colaba to the station before but suggested to Danny that we should as it was a lovely clear day. We walked along Veer Nariman Road, a wide street that would lead us there. It is a magnificent boulevard, which is being carefully restored. There is a divider through the middle where they have recently planted beautiful palm trees. Many of the buildings on both sides are being restored. Most are heritage-listed, being of Indo-Victorian, Gothic and Art Deco design. This, too, in several years will be one of the most beautiful boulevards in the world.

When we arrived at the Taj Mahal Palace Hotel, I wanted to show Danny the area around the Gateway to India where there are acrobats, snake charmers, monkeys on chains doing tricks and bears also on chains. They are all gone and now there is a fence around the entire Gateway for security.

I have mentioned previously how I would take a horse and carriage at night from Colaba through the residential streets of Mumbai. The carriages are still there but no more horses as they are now electric with the driver sitting on the front of the carriage holding a steering wheel.

I realise how this is progress and to stop animal cruelty. I agree but it certainly has taken some of the charm and magic of the old Indian culture.

When it was time to leave Colaba and drive to the airport, I asked the driver to take us the old way to the airport as I have fond memories of this drive through old Mumbai and wanted Danny to experience it. I noticed that there were no beggars on the entire drive whereas I mentioned in an earlier chapter I could virtually recognise them at every traffic light. I then realised that I had hardly seen any beggars in Colaba whereas there were always many. I asked the driver where they were and he informed me that the government had moved them to rural areas, given them a place to sleep and given their children an education.

I researched this and learnt that this is a new government directive known as 'Bhiksha Mukt Bharat', a plan by the Modi government to have thirty of India's major cities to be free of beggars by 2026. What a wonderful objective and way of removing the cruel mafia control over the beggars and offering their children a future.

So, the India I always knew has changed. Call it progress; the changes that I have mentioned in this chapter are all for the good of the country. It is now a powerhouse and progressing in leaps and bounds with the largest population in the world. It is evolving as a global player from technology to the arts.

I still enjoyed every moment of this recent journey and the progress certainly impressed me. However, India is still a land of contrasts, boasting a rich tapestry of cultures, languages, food, traditional complexities, diversity, ancient temples, palaces, snow-capped mountains in the north to tropical beaches in the south. India has endless possibilities.

India is such a welcoming country and I look forward to many more trips to this fascinating land. It will be forever in my heart.

Chapter 66

My daughter Becky studied interior design and worked part-time in Hali during her study. After completing her diploma, she wanted to stay on at Hali as she, like myself, loved the industry and the exclusive variety of products that we were introducing to Australia. For twenty-five years, she has been my right-hand person, managing the office, stock control, marketing and advertising. She has assisted in buying and joined me on many Indian and European buying trips. The only thing she hated was when we sometimes checked into a hotel and they thought we were husband and wife!

In 2012, I received a phone call from my son, Dan, who was travelling in South America. He was studying law commerce, had completed the commerce degree and decided to take a year off before finishing his law degree.

He was in South America along the Amazon where he stayed for two days with a Shaman. A Shaman is a healer and spiritual leader in many indigenous cultures, typically known for their ability to enter altered states of consciousness. Shamans in the Amazon administer Ayahuasca, a psychoactive brew, made from a combination of two plants. Ayahuasca is known for inducing a profound, altered state of consciousness, leading to intense visions, emotional release and self-reflection. After two days of taking this brew, Dan decided his future.

He called me once back in civilisation and told me that, like his father, law was not for him and that he would like to come into my business. I was so excited. I forever thank the Shaman! He flew to India to meet me; I was there with David and our carpet journey began.

For the next nine years, Dan followed my every move. He became my shadow. He would come interstate with me to visit our stores. We visited Domotex and the Indian fairs as he would accompany me on the buying trips to India. Surprisingly, his taste is very similar to mine and he would vibe on the same new collections shown to us. He was a quick learner and got on extremely well with people; he is a great salesman. He has formed a beautiful relationship with Puneet and our suppliers all respect him. We have never looked back.

Four years ago, when I turned seventy, I wanted to celebrate the India in me as everyone that I know is aware that I have travelled there extensively and that I have a strong affinity to that mystical country, so I had a big birthday bash that I called, 'A Night in Bombay.'

Everyone dressed up in Indian costumes, we served Indian food and the night was a blast. To top it off, my children, who are musical and know my love of the Beatles, performed a full set of Beatles songs. I have never felt prouder.

I believed it was now time to let go of my business and retire, passing the business over to Becky and Dan. Technology was moving too fast for me. I am not proficient with social media, websites, Facebook, Pinterest or Instagram, and this was obviously the way to move forward.

Dan became the managing director of Hali and Becky, a director. For Becky to run the company, do all the overseas travel including regular interstate stores and work full time isn't possible as she has two children approaching their teenage years, runs the household and they require a lot of her time, but she is very involved is a director and loves the business. Dan is 24/7. He lives and breathes Hali the same as I always have.

Over the past few years, Dan and Becky have built up the largest Instagram following of any Australian rug company. They have also created a magnificent website. Their marketing strategy is working, and Hali, as it was under my leadership, now remains under their leadership, the number one branded rug company in Australia. I am convinced that receiving the start I created establishing Hali, they will take the business to another level.

They insisted that I keep a smaller share to keep my mind active, assist them when needed and stay on as an advisor as they respected my experience. I am glad they did as I still enjoy Hali and can't help myself from looking at the daily figures.

They allow me the privilege of receiving the company's airline points for my time so that I may continue my passion to keep travelling. I did insist they not take India away from me and allow me to accompany Dan on some of the buying trips and fair visits.

When we visit some of my older suppliers, I sit with the father over a cup of tea and cookies while Dan and their son or daughter conduct business.

My Magic Carpet Journey was coming to an end!

Statistics show that five per cent of businesses last over thirty years. I ran Hali consistently for forty-five years and during that time, Hali has been and still is the largest Australian importer of handmade rugs from India.

As I reflect over these forty-five years, I think to myself how was this longevity possible? These are what I believe have contributed:

- I was a pioneer in Indian rugs, being the first Australian to ever import them to Australia.

- I was bold and innovative by changing the colouring within rugs shown to me to colours that were in vogue at the time.

- I didn't only buy rugs that were presented to me but also curated ranges such as Arts and Crafts, Art Nouveau, Art Deco, Himalayan, Aubusson and Shalimar to name a few.

- I kept following the trends overseas, pre-empting the change from traditional to modern, stocking more and more modern rugs, keeping me one step ahead of my opposition. My foresight was correct as modern rug sales now count to ninety per cent of all sales at Hali, a total reversal from when I first started.

- I always ensured my suppliers that whatever I purchased would be exclusive to Hali for Australia so as not to be involved in a price war.

- I researched the best locations to open stores and stressed to all my staff the importance of Hali was offering the best service to the client of any rug company.

- I was honest and never defaulted on any payments due to any supplier nor have I ever refused to accept delivery for products ordered unless they were faulty or wrong colours had been used. This is well-known in the industry.

Throughout this journey, I have spoken about some of the people I have befriended in the industry in India and around the world. Establishing these close relationships opened many avenues. In his wedding speech, Dan mentioned that he instantly noticed on his first business trip to India how well respected I was wherever we went. These strong relationships have been a big part of Hali's longevity and growth.

That answers the longevity, but one question remains. Why have I called my journey a 'Magic Carpet'? Where is the Magic?

The Magic is the two meetings that I refer to as my sliding door moments.

The first was sitting in the coffee shop in the Varanasi Hotel in 1979, reading a book on Persian carpets and at that particular moment, being approached by a friendly young Dutchman who took me to Bhadohi, introduced me to Nasrudeen and what followed.

The second was in Atlanta where I bumped into Lakshmi in the hallway, finding the Noble House collection and then searching and fortunately finding him again.

Without these two chance meetings, my entire rug journey would have been different. Maybe I still would have had longevity and success, but would it have been a Magic one? It certainly would have been a vastly different journey.

Ian's 70's Birthday

16 HOMESTYLE | THE SUNDAY AGE | SEPTEMBER 2014

TRULY FLOORED

A Melbourne family has turned the rug trade into an art form, writes Emily Day.

Dan Swart remembers growing up in a house filled with beautiful rugs and visiting his father's store as a child and playing among the stock, jumping over stacks of carpets.

The son of fashion entrepreneur-turned-rug pioneer Ian Swart, 27-year-old Dan joined the family business along with his sister Rebecca, 37, after studying law and commerce at university.

Father Ian founded Hali Rugs in 1978 after driving a Kombi van from London to Goa in India and falling in love with the beautiful local textiles.

These days Dan travels to India several times a year to source stock, while Dan and his father also travel yearly to Germany to find top-end rugs and check out the latest trends at Domotex, the massive trade fair which draws people from all around the world.

Working with family is fantastic, says Dan, as they share the passion for finding and sourcing beautiful products for people to enjoy.

While Dan's personal favourites from Hali's gorgeous range include the classic Tabriz collection – hand-knotted and hand-dyed traditional rugs – he says that Hali's contemporary offerings are hugely popular among those seeking a more modern look. Neutral-toned floor coverings such as Hali's Himalayan collection provide a muted backdrop that allows colourful vases and cushions to pop.

For those seeking contemporary rugs with eye-catching designs, Dan says Hali's Everest collection is proving to be a big hit.

"The Everest collection has been very popular for the past 18 months or so, we can't keep up with demand," he says. Featuring stunning patterns that seem to fade in places as though with much-loved wear and use, the Everest rugs are hand-knotted from 100 per cent New Zealand wool with art-silk highlights to create a decorative artistic depth of colour and design. With shades including pink, apple green and deep blue, they are decorative pieces of floor art that add class to any room.

The Swart family's passion has grown from a simple idea to having seven stores nationwide, including in Blackburn (that opened a few months back), Armadale and Richmond, as well as in Sydney, Adelaide and the Gold Coast.

Dan says that Hali Rugs offers a sense of inclusivity that other companies don't. "We have rugs starting from $500 and going all the way up to $10,000, so while we have top-end rugs

CONCLUSION

As I had mentioned at the beginning of my story, my memoir has been about a life that my friends and family do not know I have experienced.

Therefore, I haven't written about my life in Melbourne. However, it would be remiss of me not to briefly mention the following.

My life and marriage to Gina have been wonderful. We have a large social circle of friends, loving siblings, in-laws, nephews, nieces, grandnephews and grandnieces. We have had memorable times with all of them in Melbourne and have also travelled many times with different friends and extended family.

I am extremely proud of the three children I had with Gina and my daughter Becky from my previous marriage. I have now been blessed with seven beautiful grandchildren, Angus and Abbey from Becky and Josh, Harrison, Lola and Lachie from Dan and Emma, identical twins Gabe and Archie from Sophie and Tomm.

My two youngest children, Sophie and Eli never showed an interest in entering the business like their siblings. They have carved their own careers. Sophie studied professional communication at university, which led her to a career in media buying and planning. After several years, she wanted to change careers, so she went back to university. She completed a Master of Counselling, a field she now works in and enjoys. Eli studied advertising and is doing extremely well as a creative art director. All four children have beautiful partners that I adore.

Now that I am semi-retired, I plan new adventures for Gina and myself. I don't use a travel agent but carefully prepare a six-week trip during Melbourne's winter, always with new places in mind. I enjoy spending days on my computer, searching for exciting new places to visit – hotels, day tours, restaurants and planning flights, hoping to arrange them with the Hali points that are given to me.

I also plan a shorter more relaxing place to stay in March, usually on an exotic beach.

I was lucky to have been born in the time of aviation, without which I could never have had the privilege of enjoying what I have been able to do.

I hope these adventures Gina and I now go on will continue for many more years, maybe with enough stories to write another memoir.

ACKNOWLEDGEMENT

To my father who sadly became wheelchair-bound at age sixty-seven. This was the only reason that I entered the rug industry. It was never on my radar, and I'm sure had his accident not occurred to him, I would have remained in the rag trade.

He became very sad and had to reside at the Montefiore Homes Aged Home as my mother was not able to care for him.

I would often pick him up on a Sunday morning if I was working and he would spend the day with me first at the Persian Carpet Warehouse and later at Hali. He would enjoy spending these days with me and was proud of what I was achieving, particularly with Hali. I will never forget his heartfelt words one Sunday when he turned to me with his sad eyes and said in all sincerity, 'My misfortune has become your fortune.'

How true this was, and how sad his life had become. He passed away at age seventy-four about a year after I started Hali, I believe from sadness as he could never cope with being wheelchair-bound. Had it not occurred, my life would have been very different, but we can't change history.

I also wish to thank my mother, who passed away at age ninety-eight on the 25th of July, 2019, for keeping the letters that I wrote to my parents on my extended trip from 1974 to 1976. I found these when clearing her home and they certainly helped me in remembering in detail the two-year journey that began in 1974.

www.ingramcontent.com/pod-product-compliance
Lightning Source LLC
Chambersburg PA
CBHW051310110526
44590CB00031B/4358